BRITISH TOWNS

Photographs by Oliver Benn ◆ *Texts by Local Authors*

BOUVERIE HOUSE • LONDON

CONTENTS

TITLE PAGE: King Henry VI laid the foundation stone for King's College Chapel, seen here across the Backs, in 1446, but the building took 80 years to complete, because royal funds had to be diverted into warfare.

LEFT: Cornforth Hill (right) is one of Richmond's most attractive terraces of Georgian houses, fronted by cottage style gardens. In the background is the Gothick folly Culloden Tower.

FOR THAO

INTRODUCTION

by Peter Richards

Ask what makes the British town and you soon find yourself perplexed. Certainly it's not any unity of taste, traditional building materials or date – that much is clear from the magnificent diversity of buildings and townscapes savoured in Oliver Benn's evocative photographs. The bonds are subtler and more profound.

In essence, all towns are clusters of streets and houses that depend for their survival on commerce. Trade is their lifeblood: no market, no money – and no memorable buildings either. What's more, the sources of urban wealth can be surprising. Saffron Walden found prosperity in the fifteenth and sixteenth centuries growing the

BELOW: Lincoln's prosperity rose and fell with the navigation on the Brayford Pool, seen here with the cathedral in the background. Now this area is being revived by the building of the University of Lincolnshire and Humberside.

ABOVE: A galleon atop an award-winning fish and chip shop on the corner of High Street in Conwy is a reminder of the town's maritime past.

saffron crocus needed to dye textiles, Dartmouth in the sixteenth century by despatching men to fish for cod off Newfoundland.

Yet what makes the *character* of a town is a different matter. There are really three strands to it: position, planning and people.

Position because that's what defines a town's

ABOVE: Richmond Castle and town from the south east, separated from the foreground meadow by the steep valley of the Swale, the fastest-flowing river in England.

potential: who can imagine Cambridge without its river, Edinburgh without its castle rock, Brighton without its beach, Bath without its hills and crescents. Before the coming of the railways, position determined what building materials were available too. For the finest medieval buildings, like the cathedrals at Salisbury, Exeter and Lincoln, that material was oolitic limestone. For eighteenth-century town houses in Bath or Edinburgh New Town it was stone from local quarries. For the English Midlands, it was clay and timber, from the fifteenth century fired together on site in huge clamps to make bricks.

Less obvious is the fact that all the towns in this book were deliberately planned. Lincoln, Exeter and Bath began as Roman forts, Oxford

and Warwick as part of the network of Saxon fortified towns Alfred the Great established to fend off the Danes. Look at any of their town plans and you can still see the original grid of streets.

Later medieval towns were invariably military strongpoints too. In the eleventh century, as a money-making venture, Norman lords might lay out streets and a marketplace alongside their newly built castles, as they did at Ludlow and Cardiff. And when Edward I conquered north Wales, he built Conwy in a few frenzied years (1283–7) to establish a permanent English presence: not just the great castle but a planned town with defensive walls almost a mile in circuit.

Even churchmen founded towns. About 1220, the bishop of Salisbury abandoned Old Sarum, a fortified town dating back to the Iron Age, and moved his see to New Sarum – Salisbury – which he laid out ambitiously from scratch on much lower ground by the Avon. You can still walk round the great market place along streets called Butcher Row, Oatmeal Row and Fish Row.

Most important of all, as Benn's photographs remind us, it is people who in the end give towns so much of their character. Not always the best character, mind you. Even in the demure age of Jane Austen, the environmentally sensitive complained that 'beer-houses render our streets extremely unpleasant in summer' and 'black smoeks and caustic vapours [from

LEFT: The staircase leading up from the lower courtyard to the principal rooms of Plas Mawr (the "Great Mansion") in Conwy. It was built by Elizabethan adventurer Robert Wynne and had 365 windows and 52 doors.

ABOVE: The boatfloat in Dartmouth, with the seventeenth century Royal Castle Hotel and "New Quay" in the background. Originally, the cod merchants' ships could sail up to their houses on the quay.

coal fires] poison the air we breathe'. In Bath, 'filth, ashes, dirt, rubble and rubbish' defiled the streets and din was ceaseless, as the novelist herself complained: the endless carriages, 'the heavy rumble of carts and drays, the bawling of newsmen, muffin-men and milkmen, and the ceaseless clink of pattens'.

Love it or hate it, though, it's bustle like this that in the end makes a town and marks out the living from the dead, however beautiful and exquisitely mummified. It's the human factor that makes Ludlow more memorable than Lavenham, Brighton more pleasurable than Burford, for 'God made the country,' as the poet Cowper famously remarked, 'and man made the town'.

MEDIEVAL AND RENAISSANCE TOWNS

CAMBRIDGE

Text by Peter Richards

In the drug-fuelled seventies, you knew where town divided from gown in Cambridge. At a towering Victorian lamp-standard in the middle of Parker's Piece, the windswept rectangle of green that separates the city's historic, university-dominated centre from real life: the take-aways, traffic, Asian grocers and Victorian terraces that ebb fitfully away towards the station. 'Reality checkpoint' it had been labelled by some sharp-eyed

ABOVE: Cambridge punts are poled from the back, Oxford punts from the front - and it's harder than it looks. Locals see punting as the Fens' revenge on tourists. Every summer a good percentage unexpectedly end up treading icy water, then wringing out sodden Gap sweatshirts ignominiously on the bank.

LEFT: Victorian medievalism at its most exuberant in the Old Hall at Queens' College. The interior was transformed by William Morris in 1875-6, its newly revealed fifteenth-century roof timbers sumptuously painted in red and green, with gold mouldings and black-and-white stencilling on rafters and beams. Some 885 gilded lead castings in the form of stars add to the glittering effect.

ABOVE: All the most famous statues of classical antiquity can be seen as casts in the University's Museum of Classical Archaeology. On the left here is Niobe, in Greek myth a Theban queen who boasted that her six sons and six daughters made her superior to the goddess Leto, whose offspring numbered only two. In revenge, Leto sent her children, Apollo and Artemis, to kill Niobe's. The queen herself was turned into a great stone, still weeping petrified tears for her dead children.

LEFT: The Laocoön group is a masterpiece of the Hellenistic baroque, made about 200 BC and rediscovered in Rome in 1506. Michelangelo was among the first to see it. It shows the Trojan priest Laocoön and his two sons being attacked at the altar by two giant serpents, as punishment for defying the gods.

subversive, in neat yellow letters beneath ornate, cast-iron dolphins picked out in fairground colours.

These days it's different. Stoned students have given way to stripped pine as cash-strapped university families with kids and bicycles have taken over terraces built for college servants and then split in the sixties into beaten-up flats. Gone are the days of private incomes and professional

RIGHT: Trinity Great Court was created in the 1590s, in the last year of Queen Elizabeth I, the magnificent fountain in the reign of her successor, James I. The sprint, celebrated in Chariots of Fire, that is possible around the 370m perimeter path while the chapel clock strikes midday was first accomplished by Olympic hurdler Lord Burghley in 1927. The clock chimes 24 times, taking 45 seconds.

BELOW: Trinity College's predecessor, King's Hall was founded on this site in 1332 by Edward III, king of England during the Hundred Years War. The hall's warden was to receive 4d a day, and each of the 35 scholars 2d (though only when the king's representative, the sheriff, could find the money). Today, the king's memorial is this statue of 1600 below the Trinity chapel clock.

mansions in leafy west Cambridge – big, rambling buildings occupied now by the businessmen who have been the main beneficiaries of the high-tech boom that in twenty years has transformed the hinterland of this medieval market town into Europe's fastest growing region. 'Silicon Fen' looks set to rival Silicon Glen.

Even now, the world thinks Cambridge is all punts, port and privilege. Only 52 per cent of undergraduates come from state schools and formal dining at the grander colleges can still be daunting for the uninitiated: gowns and Latin grace, fine silver on starched cloths and waiters in white jackets. Remember, port circulates to the left in Cambridge, to the right only at Oxford, however.

Yet such arcane social niceties disguise the ruthless meritocracy that is today's Cambridge: where university teaching and research are ranked higher than anywhere else in Europe, where colleges fight to attract the brightest state-school students, and where the highest accolade among dons is to murmur that someone has a 'first-class mind'. More undergraduates get firsts here than at any other British university, and the boast of the richest and grandest college, Trinity, is that it has produced more Nobel Prizewinners than the whole of France. It has notched up another two, and a couple of Fields Medals

(the equivalent in mathematics) in the last eighteen months.

Much has changed, though. Cambridge is unashamedly elitist but, with rare exceptions, snobbish no longer. You don't, contrary to popular belief, get in by being born with a silver spoon in your mouth – only because of three (or better) As at A-level. But old prejudices are hard to eradicate. Undergraduates still come predominantly from the south of England. And it's true that every Thursday the predominantly Conservative Cambridge Union Society still holds mock parliamentary debates at which dinner jackets and long dresses are as obligatory for

ABOVE: Aglow with colour at any time of year is Christ's College, founded in 1505 by Lady Margaret Beaufort, the mother of Henry VII. In First Court, the dining hall on the left is mostly nineteenth-century pastiche and the Tudor buildings are masked by eighteenth-century stone façades and sash windows. The result, however, is magical.

ABOVE: Each June, Senate House Yard (foreground) sees crowds of proud parents and crocodiles of new graduates processing from their colleges in gowns and BA hoods trimmed with white fur. Behind lie the Old Schools, originally the lecture halls of the medieval university, and in the distance the stumpy tower of the university library (1934), an austere slab of plum-coloured brick.

BELOW: The stripey awnings of Cambridge market conceal the best cheese, fish and fruit in the city; in season, you can find local specialities like Fenland sweetcorn and Cambridgeshire gages (a type of plum). Far smaller now than in medieval times, it once spread east over the entire city-centre block now monopolised by colourless chain retailers.

speakers as party political point-scoring.

Dig deeper, though, and you'll hear estuary English resounding around Cambridge courts quite as often as the fruity tones of the upper classes. Ethnic minorities from inner-city schools arrive in increasing numbers, public schools complain that they are being discriminated against, and the era of bachelor dons and all-male colleges fades to vanishing point. Cambridge academics work extraordinary hours, but these days the chatter over lunch is as much about work, children and who's sleeping with whom as it is anywhere else. Don't expect wine either. Lunch at the Cavendish Laboratory – the world famous lab at which Thomson discovered the electron and Rutherford the structure of the atom – and

you'll get chips and Coke not sole and Sancerre. It's no more than a pit stop, a work canteen for working physicists.

For the visitor, this more democratic Cambridge means that the university is more accessible than ever before. The 40-acre Botanic Garden with its 8,000 species of plants celebrated its 150th birthday three years ago. Last year it was the turn of the Fitzwilliam Museum, a life affirming collection of painting and pottery, mummies and medals, displayed in comfortable,

BELOW: The backs of the best-known Cambridge colleges, including Clare (right background), are linked by the River Cam like beads on a necklace. But in the Middle Ages the river here was a commercial throughfare, with wharves at which timber, stone and food could be unloaded.

ABOVE: Monumental brick gateways emblazoned with heraldry are a notable feature of sixteenth-century Cambridge colleges like Jesus, Christ's and Trinity. Here at St John's, the figure of the saint with chalice, serpent and eagle over the gate was renewed at the Restoration at a cost of £11. The evangelist's eagle has become the symbol of the college too.

country-house surroundings in a grandiose temple of art on Trumpington Street. Like the University's equally loved contemporary art gallery, Kettle's Yard, it is open six days a week – and free to visitors, as it has always been.

Then there's the University Library, boasting 6 million books, 92 miles of shelves – and corners so remote that ancient dons could expire and gather dust for weeks before being discov-

ered. Visitors can see the best illuminated manuscripts, early maps and printed books in a new, lottery-funded display area. Indeed, you can find free exhibitions on almost any subject around the university: on archaeology and anthropology, geology, zoology, history of science, even polar exploration. Most astonishing of all is the Museum of Classical Archaeology on Sidgwick Avenue, the world's largest collection of plaster casts of Greek and Roman statues – over 600 in all. Known to generations of students as the Ark, it was conceived originally as a Victorian 'archaeological laboratory' for studying ancient art and sculpture.

Few visitors discover the 'Ark', but the same cannot be said for King's College Chapel, with its soaring fan vaults and glowing medieval glass, a universal emblem of the city that no tourist misses. On every itinerary too is Trinity Great Court with its monumental brick gateway, cobbled walks and gently splashing seventeenth-century fountain. Beside Great Gate, beneath Isaac Newton's room on E staircase, stands an apple tree descended from the one that in 1666 inspired the theory of gravity. Thackeray and Tennyson were students here, as was Byron – who kept a bear in his rooms – and the historian Macaulay, famously hit in the face with a dead cat when mistaken for the Tory candidate in a local election.

For a bird's eye panorama that stretches beyond King's and across the Cam to the hazy fields beyond, climb the tower of Great St Mary's, the university church. Behind is the colour and bustle of Cambridge market. In front lies the historic heart of the University: Senate House, to which students process in hoods and

gowns each June to receive their degrees; and the Old Schools, seat of the University's administration. Embedded in the buildings are the original lecture halls, or Schools, used by students of theology and law from the fourteenth century. The law faculty only moved out in 1996, when it acquired a gleaming, purpose-built new home of steel and glass on the University's arts campus on Sidgwick Avenue.

In the last decade Cambridge has seen a wave of award-winning buildings. In the colleges, the new libraries are most worth a look: at Clare

BELOW: Queens' College – note the apostrophe – is named after two fifteenth-century royal patrons, the wives of Henry VI and Edward IV. The President's Lodge in Chapel Court is one of the few half-timbered college buildings to survive in Cambridge. Inside is a grand, panelled long gallery for entertaining guests, its polished, broadly-planked floor impressively contorted by the years.

RIGHT: At St John's the river is spanned by the Bridge of Sighs (1831), named after its Venetian counterpart and dubbed by Queen Victoria the most 'pretty and picturesque' feature of the University. The brick ranges on the right are seventeenth century, while the extravagantly neo-Gothic New Court to the left belongs to the 1820s.

ABOVE: Established in 1584 on the site of a Dominican friary dissolved at the Reformation, Emmanuel College took over the crumbling monastic buildings as its own. The elegantly panelled dining hall by James Essex (1760-4) is an adaptation of the original Dominican church. Students eat in the body of the hall, fellows of the college and their guests at high table at the far end.

LEFT: Vividly banded in red and blue, the massive columns of the University's new Judge Institute of Management Studies (by John Outram, 1996) recall the facade of an Egyptian temple. 'Seminar balconies' zigzagging around the walls add to the theatrical feel. You would hardly be surprised to see the curtain rise for Aida. Residents of Cambridge have voted the building their favourite recent addition to the city's architectural landscape.

(1986), Downing (1993), St John's (1994), Jesus (1996) and Trinity Hall (1998). But there's also Sir Michael Hopkins' elegant Queen's Building at Emmanuel, and Richard MacCormac's chapel at Fitzwilliam, which mimics the deck of a ship.

Most arresting of all is the Judge Institute of Management Studies on Trumpington Street (1996), a theatrical confection by John Outram erected behind the Victorian façade of Old Addenbrooke's Hospital. Inside, a huge atrium soars from gleaming marble floor to tiger-striped Art Deco roof with a bravura that would do justice to a Manhattan skyscraper of the golden age – a splendid visual metaphor for the self-confidence of this medieval city.

OXFORD

Text by Stephanie McKeown

Anyone fortunate enough to find themselves walking through Oxford as the sun rises will find it easy enough to picture the city as it was a century or more ago.

Attractive as it is at any time of day or night, Oxford shows its best face to those prepared to sacrifice a few hours' sleep. Get up before the shoppers, workers and students, walk down St Giles and along Broad Street,

ABOVE: The Head of the River *pub is one of the busiest in Oxford during summer, when drinkers are joined by people hiring punts and boats. The pub is named after the finish of the colleges' annual rowing races when crews of eight (plus coxswain) chase each other up a narrow stretch of the River Thames, attempting to bump the boat in front, instead of racing side by side.*

LEFT: The vault of the Divinity School is a masterpiece of English Gothic architecture, begun in about 1420 and not completed until 1488. It is likely that Oxford architect William Orchard (d. 1504), also master mason for the chapel and cloister of Magdalen College, finished in 1478, was the designer.

peer into Radcliffe Square and go along New College Lane, by the back of All Souls and Queens', past St Edmund Hall… by the time you get as far as Magdalen you could bump into Oscar Wilde in the porters' lodge and think it nothing out of the ordinary.

Indeed, at six in the morning during term time the only thing likely to disturb your day-

dreams of an unmechanised age is the sight of squads of rowers on bicycles, gluttons for punishment, headed for early exertions on the River Thames. Other than boaties, few students are to be seen about the streets until at least ten, when a handful of the keener sort put in an appearance for lectures at the Examination Schools in High Street.

The days when it was a fineable offence for a junior member of the university to be seen about the streets without his or her academic gown are long gone and now, if you want to spot a student, you have to look for the telltale terrible jumpers, or the shadowed look of someone who has been up all night writing an essay on the rise of absolutism in Europe in the

seventeenth century. But while the uniform has changed, as have the majority of the university's most blatantly anachronistic habits, it could be argued that undergraduate life in Oxford has stayed pretty much the same since the historian Edward Gibbon talked about his idle and unprofitable days as a gentleman-commoner at Magdalen between 1752 and 1753.

The bulk of students' academic work is still based round the weekly or twice-weekly tutorial, when one or two students spend an hour reading out essays and discussing work with their tutor. This degree of close, personal supervision is still what distinguishes Oxford and Cambridge from most other universities and, while the system is profligate of both time and money, its

ABOVE: It was the poet Matthew Arnold who, in his poem Thyrsis *(published in 1867), first mentioned "that sweet city with her dreaming spires/She needs not June for beauty's heightening". In this skyline the spire of St. Mary's Church is on the right, All Souls College in the centre and the tower of Magdalen College at the left.*

many advocates argue that it remains unsurpassed as a way of exposing and addressing a student's weaknesses.

Tutorial preparation for most involves spending some time in the library, either a student's college library, a faculty library, or the Bodleian, the main university library. The Bod's collection of some six million books is housed in many different libraries, for example the Radcliffe Camera, the New Bodleian or the Law Library.

Unlike the Bodleian, college libraries nor-

BELOW: A corner of Durham Quad in Trinity College,so called because it incorporates part of Durham College, founded in the late 13th century for students from Durham and other northern monasteries.

ABOVE: Magdalen College, Cloister Quad. Magdalen (pronounced 'maudlin') was founded in 1458 and stands on the banks of the River Cherwell, one of only a handful of Oxford colleges with a riverside location.The grotesque carved animals surmounting the cloister buttresses date from the founder's time but were substantially restored in the 19th century.

mally allow students to borrow books for up to a term at a time. Many stay open into the small hours, playing host to undergraduates enduring all-night essay crises. These college libraries are not open to the public save by special arrangement with the librarians.

At first undergraduates lived in academic halls, of which only one, St Edmund Hall, still survives, but the first colleges – University College, Balliol and Merton – had been founded by the end of the 13th century.

Today there are 39 colleges scattered throughout Oxford. A college may have 200 or 300 students and each is a self-governing body with its own – often considerable – assets. All now admit men and women, with the exception of St Hilda's, the only women's college left in Oxford, and most admit undergraduates in all academic disciplines.

Typically, a student will spend at least one year living in college. In the past decade or so the colleges' response to the shortage of private rented housing in Oxford has been to build more student accomodation and it is now not unusual for an undergraduate never to have to live outside college during his or her time at

university. These days the majority of colleges allow their undergraduates in and out at any time of day or night and the students who still scramble over walls do so because they want to rather than because they have to.

One of Oxford's best-known traditions is that students have to wear sub-fusc for matriculation, graduation and university exams. Sub-fusc consists of dark suit, white shirt and white tie for men, and black skirt or trousers, white shirt and black tie for women, complete with academic gown and cap or mortar board for both sexes. During Finals in May and June visitors are either amused or appalled by the sight of hordes of students in sub-fusc pouring out of Examination Schools and holding up traffic in the High while they celebrate the end of their exams by popping champagne corks and throwing flour around.

One of the university's oddest customs is the annual ceremony at All Souls College's gaudy (reunion dinner) where the Fellows, carrying a dead duck on a pole, process round the college. It is said that they are searching for the mallard duck which supposedly flew out of a drain when the college foundations were being laid.

Education could be described as the biggest

BELOW: The Front Quad (c.1700) of St. Edmund Hall, or Teddy Hall as it is familiarly known. One of the university's smaller colleges, it is also the only medieval academic hall to survive in Oxford. The college library is now in the Norman church of St Peter in the East and the graveyard there is a popular place for summer parties.

ABOVE: Oriel College, St. Mary's Quad. The third and smallest of Oriel's three quadrangles, its mainly Renaissance style makes a pleasing variation from the more spacious Front Quad. The ubiquitous bikes, used by students and tutors alike, are also in evidence.

LEFT: The Front Quad of Oriel College. This fine example of 17th century Gothic, seen from the college's main entrance in Oriel Square, is dominated by the hall porch and the statues above it. These perhaps represent Edward II, the college founder, and either Charles I or James I, with the Virgin Mary above.

ABOVE: The Bodleian Library (left), seen from the cupola of the Sheldonian Theatre. In the right background is the Baroque Radcliffe Camera, believed to be the first round library in the country and now part of the Bodleian.

RIGHT: University ceremonies such as graduation and the award of honorary degrees take place in the Sheldonian Theatre, which was the first major work of Sir Christopher Wren. The rows of wooden benches inside, known as the hemicycle, provide notoriously uncomfortable seats for the audience at events in the theatre. Here the Chancellor's Throne is in the foreground, while one of the Orators' Pulpits is in the left background.

LEFT: New College Chapel:the figures of various Saints on the reredos behind the altar, seen here, date from the 19th century. It was William Archibald Spooner, College Warden from 1903, who gave our language the word 'spoonerism', the most famous example of which is probably Spooner's alleged rebuke to an undergraduate who was being sent down, or dismissed: "You have deliberately tasted two worms and you can leave Oxford by the town drain".

SMOKING
IS PROHIBITED
IN ALL PARTS
OF THE
SHELDONIAN
THEATRE

EXIT

industry in a city which has two universities – Oxford Brookes University is based at Headington to the east of the centre – and a further education college as well as a plethora of language schools and crammers. But manufacturing has also played a key part in Oxford's development and was the foundation of communities like Blackbird Leys and Cowley.

As traditional heavy industry has waned, companies which exploit new knowledge and research, particularly in the biotechnology field, have prospered in the city. There are also a large number of publishing houses, including the famous Oxford University Press, and many bookshops.

Oxford also has a range of other shops, four successful theatres, six cinemas, a variety of nightclubs, and quantities of attractive and idiosyncratic pubs, many of which now stay open until the small hours.

But it is possible to find refuge from all this on the river. Punts and rowing boats are available for hire during the summer on the Thames, or Isis, at Folly Bridge, and on the Cherwell at Magdalen Bridge or Cherwell Boathouse in north Oxford. A sunny afternoon spent picnicking in a punt is one of the most enjoyable pleasures the city has to offer.

LEFT: A debate in the impressive 19th century Debating Chamber of the Oxford Union, whose motions remain at the cutting edge of contemporary issues. It is also the main centre and focus for the university's student life.

RIGHT: Overview of Oxford looking west from the tower of Magdalen College, with the Radcliffe Camera (centre left) and the curving High Street.

MEDIEVAL AND RENAISSANCE TOWNS

WARWICK

Text by Jo de la Mare

O n the bank of the Warwickshire Avon the county town has its gems, valued and treasured, but worn with an unassuming grace like a dowager's diamonds which have been in the family for centuries.

Residents are never surprised when strangers enquire where to find the castle. It is almost impossible to catch a glimpse of it from the town streets and you must walk away from the town towards the river and stand on

ABOVE: During the summer months there are demonstrations of social history in the castle grounds as well as re-enactments of battles by historical enthusiasts. Old crafts attract great interest from visitors of all ages. Here the Fletcher's assistant takes a break with a mug of ale.

LEFT: Caesar's Tower and the Barbican of Warwick Castle, seen from Guy's Tower, with the courtyard to the right and the houses in Mill Street to the left. Magnificent examples of the medieval fortress, both towers were built by the Beauchamp Earls of Warwick using ransom money from French prisoners taken at Poitiers and Crecy.

ABOVE: The Fletcher in the castle grounds reminds us that the vast might of English archers was often the deciding factor in so many battles.

RIGHT: The Beltmaker is also in authentic medieval costume. Medieval garments were loose and unstructured, so the belt was an essential item of clothing. It was often also decorative and ornate, as with the examples seen here.

the bridge to see the grey stone walls rising up, seemingly out of the water. It is one of England's breathtaking views, an idyllic dream castle.

The ancient town gates, at East and West, still survive, clearly defining the old town boundaries. Between the two, along High Street and Jury Street, a run of graceful early 18th century buildings, with elegant fanlights, porticos and sash windows, replace the medieval timber frame houses which were consumed by the great fire of 1694.

The town walls have all but disappeared, much of the stone being recycled into the remarkable flurry of rebuilding during what was surely one of the finest periods of English urban architecture.

At the junction with Church Street, four elegantly detailed houses were built. These are now maintained with loving care and remind us that Church Street and Castle Street once formed the important route from the castle to the Collegiate church of St. Mary.

The eastern end of the thirteenth century church miraculously escaped the great fire, and it is here that you will discover, quietly unsung, one of Warwick's treasures, the Beauchamp Chapel, dating from 1443. Slumbering serenely in the splendour of their painted and gilded tombs are the once powerful Richard Beauchamp, Earl of Warwick, together with Queen Elizabeth 1st's favourite, Robert Dudley, his third wife Lettice and their small son, adored by Elizabeth as her "Noble Impe". This is a chapel you would expect to find in a royal palace or great cathedral.

During the rebuilding of Warwick many shrewd "gentlemen architects" saw great opportunities here. They looked for inspiration to

RIGHT: The Red Knight is a familiar and unique figure at Warwick. He and his horse have been in partnership for over 21 years and patrol the castle grounds every weekend, attracting crowds of visitors who are fascinated and entertained by his accounts of armour, battles and bravery.

London where that Great Fire of thirty years earlier was providing a model. Both conflagrations had come about due to the tinder boxes of timber and thatch, so henceforth builders were to work in brick and stone, with a fashionable classical style. Here, the grand Shire Hall

ABOVE: During the 1890s, The Prince of Wales (future King Edward VII) was a close friend of the Countess of Warwick, known to all her friends as "Darling Daisy". His bedroom was kept in readiness for his frequent visits to the castle. The adjoining room for his valet is seen here.

RIGHT: After the Civil War the castle developed into a grand stately home. The State Dining Room shows a Van Dyck portrait of Charles 1st, as well as beautiful English craftmanship in the panelling, ceiling and furniture. It is still used today for special entertaining, such as visits by royalty.

ABOVE: The "bear and ragged staff", ancient emblem of Warwick. Playful carved bears are all around you in the Lord Leycester's courtyard.

and County Gaol are typical of the work of such as Sanderson Miller and Francis Smith.

In the Market Place, the north side was effectively ruined by the only bit of 1970's concrete in the town, but the stallholders still sell their goods here every Saturday, except for twice a year when the autumn "Mop" comes to town. This was traditionally a hiring fair for farm labourers and domestic servants – who could return to the "Runaway Mop" the following week to try to find a better master. These days the job-seekers have been replaced by the thunder of amplified pop music and modern fair

ground rides. Beyond the market, shopping in Warwick is idiosyncratic. No modern malls here, but many little emporiums selling all manner of things and well worth exploration.

Near the West Gate, another treasure: the Lord Leycester Hospital where a group of timber-framed buildings lean delightfully drunkenly against each other. They date from 1383, but in 1571 were converted into a retirement home for the Earl of Leicester's old retainers. Today it is still used for exactly the same purpose and the old gentlemen, wearing the blue and black Tudor robes, show visitors the picturesque galleried courtyard, the Great Hall and candle-lit Guild Chapel where they say matins every morning. The exquisite little walled garden has recently been restored and was admired by H.M. The Queen during her last visit to the town.

The Lord Leycester is one of the many venues regularly used for recitals and concerts of all kinds, organised by the Warwick Arts Society for music festivals held two or three times a year. They attract musicians from all over the world and in midsummer culminate in two fireworks concerts held in the magical setting of the castle's Pageant Fields, by the river. They are usually given by the City of Birmingham Symphony Orchestra and always play to capacity audiences.

Outside the Lord Leycester Hospital, you are

RIGHT: The galleried courtyard within the Lord Leycester shows the original buildings on the right, with the Victorian restoration of the Master's House facing you. He and his wife look after the welfare of the residents as well as caring for the fabric and heritage of this privately owned treasure. The attractive Brethren's Kitchen serves refreshments.

ABOVE: Charities, gifts and voluntary work have enabled the walled garden of the Lord Leycester to be restored recently. We now have a beautiful living record of its development since 1540. The Victorian summer house seen here was reconstructed from the original plans discovered by happy chance.

LEFT: This row of timber frame houses is part of the Lord Leycester Hospital, a glorious jumble of buildings grouped above the medieval West Gate. It is home to retired servicemen, following the tradition set up by Robert Dudley in 1571.

BELOW: Another view of the luxuriant walled garden, hidden behind the Master's House. One of the oldest gardens in Warwick, it is now open to the public at certain times. The huge 2000 year old stone vase seen here once stood on the banks of the Nile. Behind it is a 12th century Norman arch.

inevitably drawn towards West Gate. You can still see the huge iron hinges where heavy studded oak doors once hung from the stone arches. If you are a sensitive soul, you might also detect a whiff of despair and horror lingering from the days when this was called the "Hanging Gate", where the prisoners were not only hanged but sometimes executed in more hideous ways.

From cruelty to compassion: in the shadow of the Gate are some of the almshouses which grace Warwick, some very old, others beautifully designed and recently built, but all following the example set by a famous benefactor, Thomas Oken. He died in 1573, leaving his fortune to help the poor of the town. The money from this and other legacies has been so honestly and wisely administered throughout the centuries, that today there is a very useful fund for charitable use. Oken's House is preserved in the cobbled street leading down to the Castle wall.

LEFT: Seen from St.Mary's tower, the route from the church to the castle, crossing Jury Street. The junction is marked by four splendid William & Mary and Queen Anne houses including the former Court House.

ABOVE: Mill Street runs alongside the south wall of the castle to the mill, which has served in the past to produce flour for the town and also to generate electricity for the castle. The house on the left dates from the 16th century.

RIGHT: Thomas Oken's House, near the castle wall, together with a few similar timber frame houses which escaped Warwick's great fire in 1694. This is now a Doll Museum and happily for the visitors the legendary ghost of Oken is a benign and cheerful one. The little lane to the right is locally called a "jitty".

GEORGIAN AND REGENCY TOWNS

EDINBURGH

Text by James Robertson

One could construct a very full appreciation of Edinburgh simply out of the words of one of its most famous writers:Robert Louis Stevenson. It was Stevenson who wrote of the steep and craggy Old Town spilling down from the basalt plinth of the Castle rock to the Palace of Holyroodhouse as "my precipitous city". But elsewhere he wrote of the "draughty parallelograms" of the Georgian developments, and noted

ABOVE: Looking west from Calton Hill towards the Castle. In the foreground is William Playfair's monument of 1832 to Dugald Stewart (1753–1828), Professor of Moral Philosophy at Edinburgh University. Walter Scott recalled that Stewart's "striking and impressive eloquence riveted the attention even of the most volatile student".

LEFT: The Signet Library in West Parliament Square is the library of lawyers who are members of the Society of Writers to HM Signet. This lower, original library was built in 1812–18, a nave-and-aisle arrangement with each aisle having its own saucer-dome which rises above the height of the nave's ceiling.

LEFT: The tiny, irregular interior of St Margaret's Chapel, with its chancel arch decorated with chevron mouldings. It was built by David I in memory of his mother. Ironically, its Celtic simplicity honours a woman who did much to 'root out' many of the Celtic features of the medieval Scottish Church.

BELOW: The 12th-century chapel dedicated to St Margaret (c.1047–1093), the wife of Malcolm III 'Canmore', stands at the highest point of the citadel of Edinburgh Castle.

RIGHT: Extending the full length of the building, the upper Signet Library utilises classical lines to create a wonderfully light and airy space. The central saucer-dome painted by Thomas Stothard in 1821 shows Apollo and the muses consorting with ancient and modern philosophers and poets.

how important it was to see the Old Town "planted in the midst of a large, active and fantastic modern city"; for "the two react in a picturesque sense, and the one is the making of the other".

This division is so often remarked upon that it is almost a cliché, and yet it holds a vital truth.

Stevenson may have set *The Strange Case of Dr Jekyll and Mr Hyde* in London, but its examination of dual personality was inspired by the figure of Deacon William Brodie, town councillor by day, housebreaker by night; and more generally by the character of Edinburgh itself. Unlike Glasgow forty miles to the west, Auld

ABOVE: Looking east from the ramparts of Edinburgh Castle over the red-roofed turrets and gables of the eccentric properties of Ramsay Gardens, the city stretches away past the flank of Arthur's Seat and down to the Firth of Forth.

Reekie (Old Smoky) wears its heart up its sleeve rather than on it, and as a result is often portrayed as cold, snobbish and hypocritical. Of course examples of these traits exist, as they do anywhere. But Edinburgh is also endearingly self-conscious of its mixture of gentility and coarseness, of riot and restraint. The attitude of many of its citizens to the Festival is one example: the excess of noise and colour, the regular battles over what constitutes good taste, the influx of hordes of performers and visitors, are greeted with knowing shrugs and smiles. It is

RIGHT: The Great Hall of the Royal Scottish Museum in Chambers Street has been described as a huge bird-cage of glass and iron. It is 82 metres long, its high nave spanned by stilted timber arches on iron columns. Designed by Francis Fowke in 1861, it was completed in 1875, and with its fish-tanks and airiness is a place of unexpected tranquillity.

BELOW: The Palace of Holyroodhouse, at the foot of the Royal Mile, is the official residence of the British monarch in Scotland. Originally the royal guesthouse of the adjacent, now ruined, Holyrood Abbey, it has been much added to and altered down the years and has witnessed some dramatic events, including the murder of Mary (Queen of Scots) Stewart's secretary Rizzio in 1566.

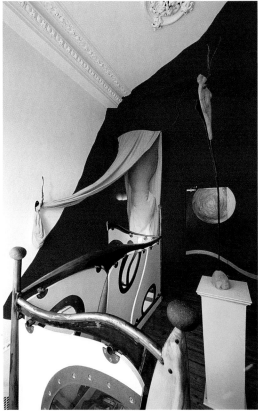

something to be tolerated, indulged, scorned, even enjoyed: but it will never, however big it becomes, upstage the city itself.

From the 12th century, when its commercial importance as a royal burgh was established, through the 15th century which saw its emergence as the political capital of Scotland, and down to the Union with England of 1707, Edinburgh was by far the most influential and populous town in the land. In the 18th century it became a hive of intellectual, cultural and economic activity, "a hot-bed of genius" as Tobias Smollett put it, illumined at various times by the brilliance of David Hume, Adam Smith, Robert Burns and a host of others. Scott succeeded to this inheritance, and it was only in

his declining years that its light faded.

This was, too, the period in which Georgian and neo-classical building, notably by the architects Robert Adam, Robert Reid, James Gillespie Graham and pre-eminently William Playfair, transformed the city, earning it the soubriquet "the Athens of the North".

Although the city continued to grow physically, it was overtaken in the 19th century by Glasgow's rapid expansion: if there was a period of relative sterility it might perhaps be found between Scott's death in 1832 and the 1930s. But with the arrival of the Festival after the Second World War, and the renewed political self-awareness of the Scots since the 1960s, that has certainly ended. A Scottish Parliament is to

LEFT: The stone staircase at 17 Heriot Row, with its display of military swords, Vanity Fair cartoons and prints by the Edinburgh caricaturist John Kay. A silver tray, complete with Royal Doulton cups and silver tea service, rests on the butler's tray, a structure traditionally used for this purpose while the butler opened the curtains in the master bedroom.

RIGHT: The drawing room in the same house. The street has long been one of the most prestigious addresses in the New Town. Built to Robert Reid's design in 1802–08, the low-profiled terraces look south into Queen Street Gardens. Robert Louis Stevenson lived here from 1857–80. This large room, uncluttered by over-ornate design, and with its specially-constructed bookcases, bright decor and comfortable armchairs and settee, manages to be both formal and relaxed.

ABOVE: The original Victorian bathroom, as installed by Robert Louis Stevenson's father around 1870, with its deep wood-panelled bath from the Edinburgh firm Rufford & Co., and one of the earliest hot and cold water systems. The original shower built over the bath also survives.

RIGHT: The house is still a single family dwelling, but the present owners, Felicitas and John Macfie, also provide hospitality for corporate and private parties. The dining-room, seen here, can seat up to thirty-six. The French Empire chandelier, although not original to the house, dates from the same period, 1802–06.

reconvene after a gap of three hundred years. The dramatic upturn in property prices which this has prompted is a sure sign of confidence in the future, and it is now astonishing to recall that as late as the 1970s a great deal of the historic centre was depressed and semi-derelict.

Indeed, if there is a danger it is that the attractions of Edinburgh both as a tourist mecca and as a place to live and work may swamp the less demonstrative side of its nature. And yet, really,

ABOVE: Arthur Lodge in Dalkeith Road. This house is unusual for Edinburgh in that it was built in the style of the Greek Revival rather than with the more typical Georgian features of its period. Known originally as Salisbury Cottage, it was built in 1827-30. Later owners included Major James Arthur, after whom the house is named. Set in exquisite grounds which include spacious lawns and a sunken Italian Garden, it was restored in 1985 as an elegant and comfortable home.

LEFT: The entrance hall or atrium, and marble staircase. The atrium, a typical Greek Revival feature, rises majestically between block-pedimented wings, and is the centrepiece of the house. It was expanded in the 1890s, but the perfectly cut and laid stone floor is original.

there is little reason to doubt the resilience of the place and its people. Much has been made of the fact that the Parliament is to meet in a new building "a stone's throw" from royal Holyrood; less, that it will be a stone's throw from what is still a lived-in and socially mixed city centre. Perhaps the mob, once so feared by courtiers and councillors, may make a come-

RIGHT: The drawing room. The ceiling design is based on that of the gates of the Parthenon. The fireplace is original, and with its Doric-styled mirror imitates the profile of the entrance porch. The deep hues of wall and woodwork give a rich but comfortable feel to the whole room.

BELOW: Detail from the dining-room ceiling. The painting by Alasdair McLeod represents Lord Byron's entrance into a Graeco-Scottish heaven. Byron died in 1824, a few years before Arthur Lodge was built.

back and keep the MSPs on their toes: as Mrs Howden put it in *The Heart of Midlothian,* "When we had parliament -men o'our ain, we could aye peeble them wi'stanes when they wer-ena gude bairns".

If this sketch seems to rely too much on lit-erature, it is because Edinburgh has inspired so much of it, and because so many writers have striven to capture the contradictions and com-plexities of the place. And if it seems strange to cast the 18th-century New Town's "present" against the Old Town's "past", rather to contrast their combined totality with the sprawling sub-urbs that surround them, it is because their shoulder-rubbing proximity speaks so eloquently of what makes Edinburgh Edinburgh. Like

LEFT: Tucked away among the Victorian tenements of the south side, this small house is reached by what appears to be a country track, as indeed it was when the house was built around 1740. Its dining-room, with original panelling and wooden cornice, was once two apartments, possibly a bedroom with dressing-room. The original stone fireplace is offset from the centre of the wall as a result. The muted colour of the panelling enhances the ornaments on mantelpiece and shelves, giving the room a simple elegance and sense of space.

London or Rome, it remains a group of villages joined into one big village – it is almost impossible to walk down Princes Street without bumping into an acquaintance, or at least recognising a few familiar faces – and yet aspires to be a city.

All the institutions of a capital exist (including the great hammerbeam-roofed hall where the old Parliament last met, which is now a magnificent waiting-room to the country's supreme law-courts) and yet these institutions are scattered with a kind of democratic disdain among the dwellings and workplaces of the general populace.

There are few cities so varied and yet so compact. In an hour you can walk from the small mountain that is Arthur's Seat to a quiet spot on the Water of Leith where a heron may be fishing, and pass en route castle, cathedrals, art galleries, department stores, a dozen splendid pubs, sweeping Georgian squares and cobbled cul-de-sacs, and much more besides. I am forced to quote Stevenson again: "You turn a corner, and there is the sun going down into the Highland hills. You look down an alley, and see ships tacking for the Baltic."

The Edinburgh of the future, culturally, politically, aesthetically, will doubtless continue to surprise us with vistas as breathtaking and as commonplace as these.

ABOVE: The main bedroom. The painted pastel-blue of the walls contrasts nicely with the rose-pink of the bathroom, creating an impression of warmth and depth.

RIGHT: This first-storey sitting-room is the only apartment which was originally built to run the full depth of the house. The Baltic pine panelling is retained, painted in a wonderfully warm yellow, and the window to the left of the fireplace has the original 18th-century shutters.

GEORGIAN AND REGENCY TOWNS

BATH

Text by Tim Bullamore

Often regarded as something of a cultural limb of London, the city of Bath has fallen in and out of favour throughout its lengthy history. Its prominence as a Roman centre was only surpassed by the Georgian era when fashionable society decamped to "take the waters" and enjoy the rich and varied diet of entertainment laid on during its 18th century heyday.

Today, as the spas are re-developed for a revival early in the third millennium, Bath can look forward to a new and meaningful golden age.

ABOVE: Looking from the east side of the river, above the weir, a favourite spot for fishing, towards Parade Gardens. Notice on the right the colonnades supporting the foundations of the city. The spire of St.John's Roman Catholic church, South Parade, is a prominent landmark.

LEFT: Pulteney Bridge, and the weir, viewed from Parade Gardens. One of only two bridges in the world to be built in this style, with shops and tea rooms along the entire length of both sides, Pulteney Bridge was erected in 1774 by the Scottish architect Robert Adam.

The city shown in these pictures is, as the visitor will discover, a melting pot of many different ages and influences. The Roman baths, only rediscovered by an inquisitive city engineer towards the end of the 19th century, have yielded many insights into the occupiers' military and leisure strategies.

Yet all around, nestling in near-perfect har-

ABOVE: The interior of the Cross Bath is where many generations of Bathonians learned to swim. Public bathing in the spa waters ceased in 1978 following a health scare, however work is taking place in order that early in the third millennium bathing and spa treatments will once again become possible. Meanwhile it can be visited at certain times.

LEFT: A dramatic view of the Roman baths taken at dusk, with the illuminated south-west corner of the Abbey in the background. Part of the Pump Room complex, and the best known of the city's baths, the lead-lined Roman remains were rediscovered by the city engineer Major Davis in 1878, having previously been extensively built over. In Roman times the baths were roofed originally by wood and later with a stone structure. The balustrade terrace and statues are a Victorian addition.

ABOVE: The Cross Bath is the smallest of the baths in the city. In 1791 Thomas Baldwin began the rebuilding of the bath as an effective visual focus to his newly colonnaded Bath Street. By 1798 the beautiful east facade, shown in this picture, had emerged.

mony, are remnants and reminders of other ages. Near to the baths stands the Abbey Church of St.Peter, part of the ancient diocese of Bath and Wells. Construction work began in 1499 and the recently cleaned interior has yielded many delights, not least intricate detail on the rare fan vaulting that makes up the ceiling.

The light coloured stone of which the abbey is constructed is to be found in almost every building of Bath and is a fundamental part of the city's character. It was quarried on a large scale to the south of the city by Ralph Allen

LEFT: The Circus remains one of Bath's most fashionable addresses. Designed by John Wood the elder (1704–1754), it is intricate in detail and perfect in execution. The Greek columns (Doric on the ground floor, followed by Ionic and Corinthian) are complemented in their seriousness by the flippancy of the stone acorns placed around the parapet. The rear of each house is completely different, a wonderful jumble of designs and fashions which today's planners would no doubt forbid.

BELOW: This fountain on Terrace Walk dates from 1859 and is by Stefano Valerio Pieroni, an Italian mason resident in Bath who as a sideline kept a public house in the city centre. This monument stood originally in Stall Street, near the baths. It was known as the "poor man's fountain" and residents and visitors were permitted to drink freely.

(1693–1764), founder of the modern postal service. His great mansion at Prior Park, with its landscaped gardens stretching down to the city, stands guard to the south of Bath.

To the north, at Lansdown, is Beckford's Tower, a folly created by William Beckford (1760–1844), author of the novel *Vathek*, and a man with too much money, too little taste and too few morals. Below here snuggles what could be termed the Georgian quarter of the city. The Circus and Royal Crescent are the most impressive buildings of the era (although there exist a further six crescents, each worthy of exploration). Both were designed by the celebrated architect John Wood, to whose eye for a gracious curve the city is interminably indebted. They are linked by Brock Street, off which can

ABOVE: The colonnades of Bath Street are now the frontage to a shopping centre but all the buildings here are, or have been, connected with the city's spas. And beneath this spot erupt the hot springs from which Bath draws her fame. To the right is the Cross Bath while in the centre are the old Royal Baths which will form part of the new spa complex opening in 2000.

be found Margaret Buildings with its delectable collection of shops.

Back in the city centre Pulteney Bridge, built in 1744 on a design for the Ponte di Rialto in Venice, is a highly original structure with shops on either side. It carries the walker across the River Avon and onto the Bathwick Estate. Erected towards the close of the 18th century for the Pulteney family, after whom many of the

The entertainment – once so vividly engineered by the city's master of ceremonies, Richard "Beau" Nash, the man who converted the 18th century city from being an unsavoury destination of ill repute to a resort of genteel manners while remaining a rogue himself – continues unabated. The impressive Theatre Royal, lovingly restored in the 1980s, offers an ever-changing smorgasbord of productions, while the multifarious restaurants – many even in this age of corporate expansion remaining independent concerns – are theatrical showcases

Right: Pulteney Bridge, with the River Avon below, from the vantage point of Grand Parade. Pleasure craft regularly ply the water above and below the weir. Across the bridge is the spacious Bathwick estate built for the Pulteney family in the late 18th century and largely unchanged today.

Below: Lovingly restored in 1980, the Theatre Royal, Bath, is regarded as one of the greatest Georgian theatres in the country. It was originally built in 1805, and is now a major player on the regional touring circuit. A studio theatre, the Ustinov Studio, was recently added to the rear of the building.

Above: Today a renowned Indian restaurant, the Eastern Eye, this remarkable hall with its three domes is situated on the first floor, above a bank, on Quiet Street. It was originally built in 1824 as an auction room. Over the years it has been used as a conference room, Methodist chapel and function room, but remains much the same as when it was first built.

roads are named, these fine mansions and adjoining streets are positively stately in their aspect. This side of the river bank is also home to a modern-day triumph, Bath Rugby, one of the game's most successful clubs.

The Victorian era's primary contribution to the city, other than a halt on the Great Western Railway (known as God's Wonderful Railway) from Paddington to Bristol, is the Empire Hotel. Some love it, others loathe it. But the Empire, today home to apartments and restaurants, is an eccentricity in a city that revels in being a little different from the norm.

And that bring us to the question of what is the character of the city? Whether a back-packer enjoying the comradeship of the city's youth hostel, a jet-setter exploiting the luxury of one of several grand hotels in or close to Bath, or a visitor manouvering between these polarities, each will find his or her own answer to that question, but character they most certainly will find with little effort.

LEFT: In the first floor drawing room of an 18th century house in the centre of Bath, the wall to the left had been completely filled in by the previous occupants. Careful rebuilding with a well-proportioned doorway leaves the viewer unaware of the modernity of the present doors. The fireplace has recently been added although the grate is from a Georgian house in Bristol. The mirror was acquired at an auction in New York for the princely sum of ten dollars.

ABOVE: This is an exact copy of a period bath and is in full working order. The fireplace remains from the original building however the dado rail was installed during the present conversion. The use of chequered flooring and plain coloured walls adds to the feeling of spaciousness in the room.

ABOVE: The kitchen of this Grade I listed house, built in 1757 to the designs of John Wood the elder, exudes a rustic charm through the use of natural woods and simple grey-blue colouring on the cupboards. It is old-fashioned in looks but modern in content.

RIGHT: The ground floor dining room shows how modern convenience can sympathetically be married with Georgian grace. In common with many of its neighbours, the house was formerly used as offices. Since 1997 the current owners have restored it to an elegant family home. The fireplace is a copy of a Georgian design and is complemented by the contemporary light fitting in the style of a pineapple. The yellow of the walls is from a National Trust paint.

LEFT: Many home owners in Bath have gone to extraordinary lengths to restore properties to how they might originally have been, while at the same time making sympathetic concessions to modern living. In the first floor drawing room of this five-storey house in Bathwick (designed in 1823 by John Pinch), the owner has had furniture made which resembles that of the late-Georgian era. Particularly worth noting are the camel back sofa and two wing chairs.

BELOW: The ground floor dining room of the same Bathwick house retains all the original features of the property, including the fireplace. The double door to the right, known as the bridal door, originally led to the parlour, but now gives onto the kitchen.

in their own right.

For 50 years the annual Bath International Music Festival in May, whose past directors have included Yehudi Menuhin and Michael Tippett, provides stimulation of a cerebral variety while its younger sister the Bath Literature Festival brings well known authors to the city in February. The Royal Photographic Society and Royal Scientific and Literary Institute add to the intellectual dimension and are complemented by the out-of-town University of Bath

LEFT: Restoring the garden of this Bathwick home to its original splendour is a recent undertaking, however the formal, late-Georgian style of a straight pathway through the middle of the lawn is clearly visible. Box hedging has been planted and will eventually flourish alongside the walls.

ABOVE: The neo-Georgian orangery at the end of the garden has been built using freshly quarried Bath stone. The sympathetic paint work and stencilling has been undertaken with National Trust paint. Orange trees, lemon trees and vines are grown inside.

with its formidable reputation in the world of science. On a lighter note, self-regulated street entertainers vie for space in Abbey Church Yard while other pedestrianised areas of the city centre draw large crowds to enjoy the famed shopping attractions in a city partly devoid of multi-national chain stores.

The bohemian quarter of Walcot provides a spiritual and actual home for impoverished artists and musicians. The Saturday morning flea market held in a former tram shed, one of many in

LEFT: *This distant view of Bath was taken from the steps of what is now Prior Park College. The gardens falling away in the foreground were designed by Capability Brown for Ralph Allen who amassed a fortune from quarrying and postal enterprises. Just visible at the apex of the grass is a rare Palladian bridge built in 1755 above a series of fish ponds.*

RIGHT: *Prior Park College. Built by Ralph Allen, its prominent position provides exquisite views over the gardens below and the city beyond. Today Allen's former home at Prior Park is a prominent Catholic school.*

the region, is legendary, while royalty and show-business personalities regularly mingle with bargain hunters in the nearby workshops and restoration yards. That they can do so unhindered is a reflection of the relaxed and liberal atmosphere that makes Bath such an interesting and remarkable city to live in, to work in and to visit.

The city's buildings are adorned with plaques reminding the visitor of those who have visited and chosen to stay, not least Jane Austen, Admiral Lord Nelson and Thomas Gainsborough. The diarist Samuel Pepys, the composer Joseph Haydn, the poet John Betjeman and Emperor Haile Selassie of Ethiopia are among others who have chosen to spend time in the city.

The much commented upon and highly attractive floral decorations visible on the streets and in the parks are a post-war addition to the city's scenery and, despite the ebb and flow of political support, have contributed to Bath being awarded the Britain In Bloom title on several occasions.

It may only be a small, compact city, but nevertheless a city is what Bath is, with all the infrastructure and cosmopolitan diversity the visitor expects from one of the world's most famous destinations. Whatever the season and whatever your purpose for visiting, Bath stands with open arms to greet, inspire and delight those whose choose to explore her magnificent beauty, rich history and vibrant community.

BELOW: *Viewed from Beechen Cliff, a craggy outcrop to the south, this classic view shows Bath nestling in the hills. In the foreground and to the right are the Abbey and the former Empire Hotel.*

GEORGIAN AND REGENCY TOWNS

BRIGHTON

Text by Eugénie Hill

Along the wide sea front between Kemptown at the eastern end and Hove's Brunswick Town to the west is strung a necklace of priceless Georgian and Regency architectural gems, for which the astonishing Oriental fantasy, the Royal Pavilion a few hundred yards inland, may serve as a dazzling centrepiece.

Brighton wears these jewels casually. The visitor will find here no hushed, museum-style reverence, no stultified preservation of former glo-

ABOVE: Elegant Sussex Square faces four acres of private gardens. It formed part of Wild and Bushy's ambitious 1820s Kemptown development. Originally a total of 250 houses was envisaged but the final plan cut this to a more modest 106.

LEFT: Royal Crescent, built in 1798, was the first block of housing in the town to face the sea. The 14 timber-framed residences are faced with black glazed mathematical tiling. Actors Laurence Olivier and John Clements once owned houses here.

LEFT: The interiors shown here are of a sensitively restored, privately-owned first floor mansion flat in Sussex Square and illustrate a number of original features. This spacious drawing room boasts an original fireplace flanked by double pilasters. The striking red silk damask wallpaper is characteristic of the Regency period.

RIGHT: The arched, mirror-lined hall, here providing a glimpse of the drawing room beyond, has an original grand staircase rising from it.

BELOW: This sitting room also once formed part of the hall which housed the grand staircase. Note the original cast iron fireplace with its mirror-backed overmantel.

ries. The most distinctive of British seaside towns continues to defy classification and remains constantly in flux. A feisty old girl with a past both magnificent and scandalous, the town kicks up skittish heels and enthusiastically embraces everything which is new.

The origins of the place, like those of many a light and lively woman with a colourful past, were modest. The storm-battered medieval fishing community of Brighthelmstone huddled in and around the network of central alleys which

evolved over the centuries into the cheerful, commercially-thriving tourist mecca which is today's Lanes.

It was not until the middle of the eighteenth century that this obscure provincial settlement caught the eye of Doctor Richard Russell. Once he drew attention to the benefits to be derived from bathing in and drinking sea water, entrepreneurial spirits were quick to take advantage of the publicity his learned dissertations generated. Brighton's first great period of architectural and social developments was soon under way.

The final third of the century brought the town her most illustrious admirer. The dashing young heir to the throne, always a man with an eye for a fresh conquest, arriving on a visit to his uncle the Duke of Cumberland in 1783, was

ABOVE: The Royal Pavilion is instantly recognisable and has a fairy-tale allure when floodlit. The busy and attractive surrounding gardens have recently been effectively restored to their original design.

RIGHT: Hove's Brunswick Square was completed in 1830 by builder Amos Wild and his architect partner Charles Bushy. The square is one of the earliest examples of the great Brunswick Town development. Today its lawns provide a pleasant space to relax within sound of the sea.

himself conquered. Falling immediately beneath the sea siren's spell he was soon occupied with plans to build for himself a two-storey villa on classic lines.

By the eighteen-twenties, when the Prince had attained his Regency, he hankered after something more extravagantly lavish. John Nash

provided it. A remarkable, Indian-inspired exterior was devised to echo the exuberant Orientalism within. Never before nor since has such an exotic plant flourished in an English seaside garden.

The Prince Regent's patronage imbued the town with more than a hint of the racy and the raffish which has never been lost. Soon Victorian railway navigators were tunnelling through the South Downs and Brighton opened hospitable arms to humbler folk. Tens of thousands of day excursionists swarmed in. Hungry for sun and for fun they dipped cautious toes into the waters Dr Russell had extolled, before strolling along Palace Pier where gilded domes and airy minarets echoed the fantastic roofscape of the palace in Pavilion Gardens, beyond the crowded promenade.

Brighton today, having at last attained, with Hove, the status of a city, remains as lively and

RIGHT: The glowing interior of one of the most classically graceful of Brighton's many notable churches, Saint John the Baptist, in Kemptown, built in 1835.

BELOW: The Memorial Tablet shown here is dedicated to a celebrated parishioner, the beautiful and virtuous Maria Fitzherbert. Wedding rings from her three marriages, the last and most famous being that to the Prince of Wales, later George IV, are picked out in gold leaf.

ABOVE: : The remains of the neo-classical Royal Spa, opened in 1825, now form part of a nursery school. The surrounding Queen's Park was at that time a fashionable pleasure ground and is still very popular with local residents.

RIGHT: Just the place to sample the fabled Brighton air! Palace Pier, first opened to the public in 1899, has proved enduringly popular. Free admission, together with a mix of original features, ensures that it continues to pull in the crowds.

ABOVE: Brighton Marina was conceived in the early seventies as a city by the sea, and has since gone through a number of mutations. From the outset it provided a busy boating haven and over the years a number of shops, restaurants and entertainment complexes have been added. Development is ongoing and the recently completed Georgian-style housing illustrated here, at the eastern end of the marina village, has proved very popular.

as forward-looking as ever. In spite of some evidence of depredations and mistakes of judgement which purists will abhor, much of the best from the past lives and breathes alongside the present. A long tradition of music, theatre, literature and art of all kinds is maintained, often in innovative forms. This reaches its zenith each May with the world famous Brighton Festival which every year grows more wide-ranging.

Meanwhile, between the piers, down on Fisherman's Hard, a museum has been established in tribute to the town's earlier inhabitants, whose descendants' boats and nets are still in evidence spread out along the shingly beach.

For breathtaking views from the town's most gracious age you need only walk along Hove's spacious, sea-fringed lawns. Or take a trip on Magnus Volk's electric railway. The doughty Victorian engineer's most enduring enterprise still trundles eastwards from Palace Pier, nowa-days in the direction of the bustling and constantly developing Marina.

Go along the west jetty there and look landward. Cubitt's impeccable stucco terraces, crescents and squares still delight the eye.

This is a town for all men and all seasons. On a day when the sun sparkles on the sea, beneath skies as blue as when Constable painted them, it is the place to be. What is your pleasure? A stroll along the prom? A tour of the Royal Pavilion? A day at the races? Haute cuisine? Or a paper of chips – with a doze after in one of the serried ranks of deck chairs whose canvas is stirring in the breeze? Whatever your fancy, Brighton beckons... Brighton waits.

SALISBURY

Text by Roger Croft

The city of Salisbury is renowned throughout the world for its mighty cathedral and magnificent cathedral close. For more than 700 years it has also been the spiritual and commercial centre of its region.

The cathedral was built in the 13th century and the graceful spire reaching 404 feet is the tallest in England. Even more striking is the fact that the main building was constructed in a mere 38 years. This helps to

ABOVE: Myles Place, No. 68 The Close, is affectionately known in Salisbury as 'The Jewel In The Crown'. It was originally built in the 13th century but was demolished and re-built in 1720. This exceptional Georgian house is unusual in that its entrance front is faced with white stone while the rear of the house, seen here from the garden, has a red brick finish.

RIGHT: The North Gate, flanked here by High Street shops, is the main point of entry into the cathedral close, and is locked every night. It was built around 1340, and originally housed a small jail for those convicted of misdeeds within the close.

explain its unique purity and uniformity of style (Early English Gothic).

Inside the cathedral is the 600 year old 'faceless' clock, almost certainly the earliest working mechanical clock in the world. With no face or hands, it can only strike the hours, but it is still in working order.

Adjacent to the cathedral is the Chapter House. The Purbeck marble columns and distinctive fan vaulting of this octagonal building make it one of the best examples of Gothic architecture in England. One of the four surviving original texts of the Magna Carta is exhibited inside. The name 'Chapter' stems from the practice of reading a chapter of the Bible there, at meetings of the cathedral clergy.

Maintaining the cathedral is the task of the Cathedral Works Department. Here, highly skilled craftsmen and women work all the year round to ensure that all aspects of the cathedral

ABOVE: The dining room of Myles Place, showing the heavy claret red walls as favoured in the Georgian period. These make a pleasing contrast with the pale yellow colour scheme of the adjacent saloon.

LEFT: Recently restored, the hallway reflects the ornate and colourful style of the Georgian period. Plaster moulds were commonplace in wealthy homes in the 18th century and the delicate gold leaf designs, combined with the bold colours of the walls and furniture, create a dramatic effect.

RIGHT: The saloon faces the rear of the house, overlooking the tranquil gardens and the River Avon. Traditionally used by the ladies when the gentlemen had retired to the smoking room, the saloon is typically decorated in pale, fresh colours.

are constantly restored. They now use state of the art electrical tools and diamond-edged circular saws, as well as traditional implements that have changed very little since medieval times.

But today, it is the houses of the close as well as the cathedral that attract visitors. Hemmed in by a mighty stone wall, they were originally built for the canons and clergy. These impressive and ornate houses are now mostly privately owned through leaseholds, and are some of the most beautiful and sought after properties in the country.

No description of Salisbury's close would be complete without a few words on one of its most famous houses, Myles Place, described by Sir Nikolaus Pevsner as 'the stateliest 18th century house in the Close'. Beautifully restored,

both the interior and exterior offer a most distinctive example of Georgian architecture. And after painstaking work over many years, the gardens to the rear of the house, running down to the River Avon, are equally delightful.

The houses of the close include several designed or remodelled by distinguished architects, including Cathedral Clerks of Works like father and son Thomas and William Naish, Francis Price, author of the earliest architectural treatise on the cathedral, and, latterly, William Butterfield, Sir George Gilbert Scott and Thomas Henry Wyatt. Within the close Constable painted some of his celebrated views of the cathedral.

Although the cathedral and the close have survived relatively unscathed, some of the pubs

and inns of Salisbury have been modernised and refurbished to create a colourful nightlife in this peaceful city, which has a fascinating way of combining its religious background with its need for development. Haunted by tales and legends that have been passed down through the centuries, churches, chapels and vicarages have been converted into nightclubs and bars. For example, a non-conformist chapel in Milford Street has now become a nightclub, appropriately named *The Chapel*.

However, tradition lives on in pubs such as the *Haunch of Venison*, which boasts, perhaps unwisely, of having one of the smallest bars in the country. Not only is the whole bar area no bigger than your average front room, but there is also a real severed hand on display, holding some eighteenth-century playing cards, perhaps as an example of Salisbury's rough justice for cheats and miscreants.

Salisbury is now however gaining an enviable status as the artistic centre for the region. The Salisbury Festival takes place every year during the last week in May and the first week in June, attracting international performers. Acrobats, poets, musicians and dancers descend on the city and dazzle it in a blaze of colour and artistry, entertaining visitors and residents alike.

For those whose prefer a slightly more static form of art, there are many art galleries and museums. The Salisbury Arts Centre, itself built within a former church, displays many modern works while the Salisbury and South Wiltshire

LEFT: A stained glass window which has been re-leaded by the specialist craftsmen in the cathedral workshops.

ABOVE: The medieval Doom Painting in St. Thomas' Church, near the Market Square. In the centre is Christ in Majesty, flanked by representations of the Kingdom of Heaven (left) and the terrors of Hell (lower right). In medieval times when few people could read, church walls were often painted thus.

Museum focusses on the past. An outstanding example of medieval wall painting can be seen in St. Thomas's Church, near the Market Square in the city centre.

But although some things have moved forward, others remain characteristic of the city and its history. The market place in the city centre is still the site for Salisbury's market, which has taken place every Tuesday and Saturday since 1361. Traditional stalls are still popular, such as the butchers and fishmongers, but they now stand alongside jewellery designers and fashion stalls.

LEFT: *The Matron's College in the cathedral close was built in the 17th century, possibly to the designs of Christopher Wren, to provide sheltered housing for ten widows of the clergy. It is still used for this purpose.*

RIGHT; *The hexagonal 15th century Poultry Cross is the only survivor of the four medieval market crosses which marked the separate areas where poultry, livestock, cheese and wool were traded. The top was added in 1852.*

BELOW: *The* Pheasant Inn *in Rollestone Street. This atmospheric 15th century inn, with its original cobbled courtyard, incorporates the 16th century Hall of the Shoemakers' Guild.*

Street names such as Fish Row, Butcher Row, Ox Row and Oatmeal Row reveal where these various goods were sold in the medieval market. The Poultry Cross, a large stone dome-like shelter situated in the city centre, identifies the spot where poultry was traded, and it is still a favourite meeting place today. Residents of Salisbury in the 14th century would only have had a short walk from their beloved market to Love Lane, the medieval 'red light' district to the south east.

From the beautiful stately houses of the close to the lively commerce of the Market Square, Salisbury perhaps represents the most peaceful and fascinating cathedral city in England.

CATHEDRAL CITIES

EXETER

Text by Hazel Harvey

Exeter is the county town of Devon, with medieval cathedral, pink-brick university, law courts, libraries and theatres. Museums, art galleries, markets and the regional headquarters of many agencies and businesses are also to be found here. From 1537–1974 the city was proud to be a county in its own right. Its inhabitants now number about 100,000, swollen in term-time by about 10,000 students.

ABOVE: The Cathedral and North Tower from the East: since 1484 the North Tower has housed the great four-ton clock bell Peter, the oldest bell of its weight in the British Isles. It has not swung since 1676 but strikes to tell the hours, and to announce the curfew every evening at dusk, when the citizens were formerly required to go indoors, to cover the fires on their hearths.

LEFT: Mol's Coffee House: Cathedral chantry priests were housed here until the Reformation. It was later leased to an Italian shipowner, Thomas Mol. The Devon sea-dogs Raleigh, Drake, Gilbert and Hawkins met here to gather news as horsemen arrived from Plymouth or London. It later became a coffee house and then an art gallery.

The site was determined by the invading Romans when they built their camp on a plateau above the River Exe in about AD 55. A Roman city followed; protective walls were added in about AD 200. These walls have been attacked, besieged, strengthened, extended or pierced by modern roads, but they still largely encompass and demarcate the city centre. It is entertaining and instructive to walk past a section of the walls, identifying the square purple volcanic blocks cut by Roman masons, the anglo-saxon limestone castellations put up against the Vikings, the Norman curtain-walls of Rougemont Castle and the later infills of

ABOVE: The 17th century tomb of Lady Dodderidge, whose husband sat on the King's High Bench. She leans on her right forearm, wearing a fashionable hood and flowered gown and holding a laurel-wreathed skull and a prayerbook.

ABOVE: Six and a half centuries ago all the carving was as sharp as this demi-angel on the West Front of the Cathedral, which Simon Verity copied from an angel at Wells in 1982. The same artist provided the naked statue of St Peter the fisherman at the apex of the West gable.

RIGHT: Dragon Boat racing, with crews of about twenty trying to keep in time with the beating of their drummer, originated in China where it has a 2,000 year-old history. Here the frenzied activity during the summer Exeter Festival contrasts with the timeless Georgian Colleton Crescent on the clifftop, built in 1802–1803.

ABOVE: The Tudor House has foundations from 1450, was rebuilt in 1628, and meticulously restored with 17th century materials and techniques by William Lovell in 1965–1975. It has cobblestone floors, brick side walls and a slate-hung front wall incorporating wreathed heraldic devices.

softer pink Heavitree stone or even 20th-century brick. Children like to touch something the Romans touched.

Exeter has many other authentic survivals from past centuries: the Norman gateway of the Castle, the arched stone bridge from the early 1200s, the unparalleled Gothic stonework of the Cathedral, and the 18th century Custom House on the Quay. Its domestic architecture spans a succession of periods and styles, from medieval to the 20th century.

Nowadays we travel great distances so easily that we forget how dominant the regional cities

LEFT: The roofless chapel of St Catherine's Almshouses, which had sheltered twelve poor men since 1440, has been retained in a ruined state as a reminder of the 1942 Blitz. A thousand years before it was founded, a Roman town house with mosaic floors stood here.

were until recently. When it took an hour to walk in from a village on the estuary, or to bring a cartload of produce to market from a farm, or it took half a day to ride in from a country estate, the city had to provide for all local economic, legal and cultural needs.

St Boniface came to the abbey school as a small child (not yet a saint) in about 690 AD. The anglo-saxon monastery was a major source

BELOW: Stepcote Hill, the old main approach from the river-crossing to the markets in the town centre, has a cobbled section for wagons and pack-horses, with steps each side. The old timbered houses have doors to their upper floors on the steep street.

ABOVE: No.7 and 8 The Close: The cathedral canons did not live communally; each had a house on the north side of the Close. No.7 (left) now houses the Devon and Exeter Institution for the Promotion of Science, Literature and Art. In no.8, the Law Library, 18th century bow windows top the red stone of the medieval front wall. Inside, there is an extraordinary hammerbeam roof where angels appear to fly out bearing painted shields.

of learning, copying manuscripts in its *scriptorium*. The city was a particular favourite of the anglo-saxon kings. Aethelred began the royal custom of making a 'morning-gift' of the city to his bride: on the morning after their wedding night he created her Lady Paramount of Exeter, which entitled her to a share of the city's

income. In 1050 the bishop's seat was moved from Crediton to the safety of the walled city. The Bishop's Library today houses many treasures but perhaps the greatest are the *Exon Domesday* and the *Exeter Book of Anglo-Saxon Poetry*, which includes the famous riddles, 96 of which survive. They tease, suggesting rude answers, e.g. "What does a woman hide under a cloth, but it grows bigger and bigger? Not a pregnancy but a rising loaf of bread."

For many centuries the wool trade brought riches to the city's merchants as they exported cloth and their ships came home with wine and spirits, sugar and tobacco. They built fine shops in the main streets, decorating the living quarters above with elaborate panelling and carved

LEFT: Tin Lane Community Centre has been enhanced and saved from graffiti with a mosaic covering, showing the groups of all ages which meet there. Elaine M. Goodwin, an Exeter artist with an international reputation, worked on it with her students in 1987-9. Every old couple passing by think they recognize themselves among the Bingo numbers.

ABOVE: The E-shaped manor house of Cowick Barton was built from the stones of the former priory in about 1540. During the following four centuries its occupants included the artist John White Abbott (1763–1851), who restored the old house. It has been a restaurant and pub since 1963.

ABOVE: The former Schoolroom in Cowick Barton. 'I press toward the mark' (Phil.3.14) is probably not a cryptic reference to opening a priest-hole or smuggler's passage, but an admonition to strive for improvement. Resident Robert Pate left money in 1687 for poor local children to be taught here.

façades. Just outside the city walls the curving green of Northernhay was made into England's first public pleasure garden in 1612. It is still a delight, only a step away from the High Street shops, full of unusual plants and shrubs, with panoramic views of the surrounding hills. In 1772 the *Exeter Flying Post* said that the opening of the turnpike roads had brought 'families of Fortune and Distinction' to settle here. Georgian terraces and crescents were built to

house them.

An active Civic Society campaigns vigorously to retain Exeter's distinctiveness. The western High Street with its Tudor frontages and 800-year-old Guildhall survived the 1942 Blitz, but when the bombed eastern half was rebuilt with a much wider carriage-way there were plans to push this further at the expense of some of the 16th-century buildings. Professor W.G.Hoskins, the well-known historian, native of Exeter, co-

founder of Exeter Civic Society, put a stop to this, and also to the proposed demolition of the Victorian Higher Market in Queen Street. Instead, its solid granite columns and pillars were incorporated into the Guildhall Shopping Centre, lending gravitas to an otherwise undistinguished development.

The Exeter Festival in July includes performances by world-class visiting orchestras and artists, but also acts as a showcase for local societies and clubs. For the Lammas Fair young schoolchildren dance along the High Street and on the Cathedral Green. The city pays a retainer to the re-formed Second Augustan Legion to parade in Roman gear on special occasions marching in step, *sinistra dextra, sinistra dextra…*

A bonus for visitors is the guided walk service provided free by volunteer Redcoat guides. Exeter has so many treasures hidden away in addition to the obvious beauties of the Cathedral Close. The walks allow visitors to enjoy the gardens of the Bishop's Palace, the Catacombs built in 1835 below the city walls, St Nicholas Priory (Norman vaults, medieval kitchen, 15th-century guest hall, Tudor ceilings), the historic Quayside and the University grounds.

Exeter's system of medieval underground passages is unique in Britain, built to bring piped water from the eastern ridge to the cathedral canons, monks and citizens. They were first documented in 1226, but they may have originated in Roman times, when water was brought in for the Legionary Bath House. The passages were enlarged for easy maintenance and are open for conducted tours.

Throughout the year, even on Sundays now, shoppers throng the High Street. It is car-free now but blocked instead by minibuses, telephone kiosks, trees and substantial raised flower-beds. On winter afternoons the orange globe of the setting sun fills the western end of the High Street. It reminds us that it must have guided our prehistoric predecessors as they traversed southern England by the Icknield Way to reach the easy crossing of the River Exe.

LEFT: George's Meeting in South Street. Religious dissenters in Exeter included wealthy wine and wool merchants, such as the Unitarian Baring and Bowring families, who founded this place of worship, named after the new King, in 1760. It was used for services until 1987 but is now an antiques market, its goods displayed in the listed galleries and around the historic pulpit and desk.

ABOVE: One of Exeter's oldest churches, St Petrock's was formerly the parish church for the Guildhall. Now no congregations live in the city centre; the spare space is used as a day centre for the homeless, offering hot meals, showers, laundry, changes of clothes and sundry advice.

BELOW: The tomb of Edmund Stafford, Bishop of Exeter 1395–1419 and Lord Chancellor to Richard II and Henry IV, stands beside the Lady Chapel and bears his alabaster effigy in pontifical dress, with mitre and ring, hands clasped in prayer; pet dogs warm his feet.

CATHEDRAL CITIES

LINCOLN

Text by Carol Bennett

It is impossible to visit Lincoln without seeing the cathedral, if only from a distance. Whether your first glimpse is on a train coming from the south, rounding a bend in the track before pulling in to Central Station (when you see its vast shape sprawled lengthwise on the hill), or whether you look at it from the west on the bypass (where it seems to fold up like a fan, its three towers jutting up into the sky), Lincoln Cathedral is unmiss-

ABOVE: Exchequergate is a 14th-century entrance to Minster Yard through the Close Wall. The curfew bell still tolls from the cathedral, but the gates which were once locked each night are gone. Beyond, Lincoln Castle's walls and towers can be seen.

LEFT: The cathedral towers over picturesque Castle Square. Lincoln's annual German style Christmas Market has a perfect backdrop here. On the left, the Tourist Office occupies a timbered house. Straight ahead, the name of the Magna Carta public house refers to Lincoln's copy of the 1215 charter, one of only four surviving originals.

able. It presides over the city, a presence commanding the skyline. It gets into your photographs even if you don't mean it to. It seems never to change, yet it has many moods. Modern flood-lighting enhances the building in a way previous generations never dreamt possible. But it is even more atmospheric in the fog, when it can disappear from view while the lower part of the city is clear. Best of all is on a spring or autumn day, after a shower of rain, when a block of sunlight breaks through the clouds and lights up the warm, golden stone against a steel grey sky, and you catch sight of this effect from three or four miles away. It can make your heart sing. Love it or hate it (and not everyone loves it), the cathedral is a fundamental part of Lincoln's character.

Yet Lincoln had a long history before Christian times, stretching back to the late Iron Age. The Romans built a fortress, then a retirement settlement for the Ninth Legion in the first century AD. Lincoln is derived from the old name for the River Witham, the *Lindis,* and *colonia.* The settlement prospered, centred around a forum in the upper city. The most noticeable Roman survival is Newport Arch, part of the north upper city gate which still has traffic going underneath it. But an impressive chunk of the Roman basilica wall is tucked behind a hotel, and is not so easy to find. Much of Lincoln's past is hidden and not tourist-friendly. A Roman hypocaust lies beneath a man hole cover in a drive, and trun-

LEFT: A stone's throw away from the tourist buses is this large private garden behind one of the Close houses. Entering it is like stepping into another age, where Georgian elegance contrasts with the majestic Gothic architecture of Lincoln Cathedral.

ABOVE: Lincoln Cathedral's high altar stands in the Angel Choir, consecrated in 1280. So many pilgrims sought miracles at the shrine of St Hugh, who began the rebuilding of the cathedral in the Gothic style, that the east end was extended to accommodate the crowds.

RIGHT: "And the light shineth in darkness; and the darkness comprehended it not." (John 1:5). Sunlight streams through one of the Cathedral's stained glass windows onto the deserted nave, almost like flowers strewn on a grave.

cated columns of the Roman forum are in the cellar of a private house in Bailgate.

At the time of the Norman Conquest, William the Conqueror recognised the strategic advantage of Lincoln's Roman walls for both a cathedral and a castle. In 1072 he instructed Bishop Remigius to move his see from Dorchester-on-Thames in the extreme south of the huge diocese, to Lincoln in the extreme north. The centre of the west front of the present cathedral survives from Remigius's building, which was substantially complete in 1092. Disaster struck in 1185 when an earthquake toppled the Norman cathedral, but seven years later the new Bishop, St Hugh of Avalon, began

rebuilding even more magnificently in the Gothic style.

Lincoln's cloth trade had made the city wealthy. But the Black Death in the mid-14th century, and the loss of the wool staple (a tax on goods passing through the city), contributed to the city's decline. Gradually, trade became more difficult as the Brayford and Foss Dyke silted up. Having once been one of the most important cities in England, Lincoln's downfall is summed up in a 17th-century proverb : 'Lincoln was, London is, York shall be.'

The Industrial Revolution revived Lincoln yet again. The agricultural machinery and engineering works swelled the population sevenfold to 50,000 by the end of the 19th century.

Now a city of 82,000, Lincoln has seen another period of regeneration in the 1990s. Old warehouses and engineering works are being converted to accommodation for students from the new University of Lincolnshire and Humberside, De Montfort University, North Lincolnshire College and Bishop Grosseteste College. Heavy engineering is giving way to the silicon chip, and firms like GEC Plessey Semiconductors. The Lawn, an old lunatic asylum founded in 1819 along enlightened lines in a Regency mansion, has been restored, and now offers a museum, a recital hall, and a mini rain forest housed in the conservatory honouring the Australian botanical interest of Lincolnshire's own Sir Joseph Banks. The

LEFT: 'Queen Anne front, Mary Anne behind' is often said of the houses of Minster Yard. The charming private courtyard with a cathedral view seen here has been made out of the old chantry house yard with its outbuildings.

RIGHT: This 14th-century house in Minster Yard was the home of chantry priests, who offered Mass in the cathedral for the souls of the dead until the Reformation. In the 1840s a tenant altered the house, replacing some genuinely medieval features with Victorian Gothic ones, such as the leaded windows lighting the staircase, and the medieval style timber roof.

ABOVE: Many Minster Yard houses have upstairs drawing rooms like this one in the former chantry house. The room was once nearly twice its present size, connected to the next room by an opening between the columns, and ending in a medieval oriel facing the cathedral.

Museum of Lincolnshire Life, the Usher Gallery, and the Cathedral Library have changing exhibitions and events. The Waterside Shopping Centre and the redeveloped shopping area at the old St Mark's Station site, the many new pubs and restaurants, and a multi-screen Odeon, are all recent attractions. The area's music lovers enjoy the Schidlof Quartet, and an annual visit of English Touring Opera at the exquisite Theatre Royal. The cathedral's own choral services, and the concerts put on there, are an

LEFT: Anyone climbing the aptly-named Steep Hill can appreciate why Lincoln is divided into 'uphill' and 'downhill' areas. As the term implies, uphill is considered to be a more desirable neighbourhood, including as it does Minster Yard and the cathedral.

RIGHT: Looking down Steep Hill, with the Harlequin Galleries on the right. Timber framed, stone, and brick buildings, all jumbled up, add to the charm of this part of Lincoln. The shops vary from a specialist teddy bear emporium to a pottery providing hand-made replicas of medieval wares.

LEFT: A rare survival of a medieval bridge with shops still on it, the Norman High Bridge once also supported a chapel dedicated to St George. From one of the timber framed shops, dating from around 1600, wafts the delicious aroma of freshly ground Stokes coffee.

RIGHT: The Waterside Shopping Centre, opened in 1992, was built alongside the River Witham, downstream from the High Bridge. This area was the waterfront from Roman to medieval times, and would have been as busy with water-borne trade then, as it is now with shoppers and pleasure craft.

ABOVE: Rus in urbe. Malcolm Withers and his partner Lorraine enjoy the best of both worlds: they live in a period house set in a country garden which is in the heart of Lincoln. The older, lower part of the house is to the right. In 1773 a coal merchant refaced the other end of the house, giving it an ashlar stone front worthy of a gentleman's residence.

BELOW: On the top floor, the 'cottage' feel of parts of the house is in evidence. A bold use of colour in unusual combinations was inspired by the National Trust paint range. Malcolm did most of the building work and Lorraine painted during a hectic eighteen months of renovation.

important part of the cultural scene.

Perhaps because of its distance from London, Lincoln is good at making its own amusements. Among many amateur groups, the Lincoln Shakespeare Company is like a breath of fresh air, young and innovative, and willing to turn out on a cold wet evening in the Bishop's Palace. For its size, Lincoln does very well. And that's part of its charm. It's intimate. It's unusual for a local to walk around Lincoln without meeting a friend. Some might find that oppressive, but most people who like Lincoln enjoy the small-town feel of the place. It isn't flooded with tourists, although there is plenty of historical interest here. To add to that, there is unspoilt countryside to explore within sight of the city. You can walk everywhere in Lincoln, and you can walk out of it.

A county town and a cathedral city, now with its own university. A city of contrast, where the

ABOVE: Gracious living once required a staff below stairs to serve at elegant dinner parties in this dining room. Lorraine and Malcolm took the brave step of reinstating the basement kitchen, where there were not one, but two cast iron ranges. Their wine is stored in a subterranean wine cellar.

RIGHT: Lorraine and Malcolm were delighted to find that so many features had been preserved in their house. It was formerly occupied by an elderly eccentric artist, who made few changes. All the original woodwork survives, such as the handsome arched niches in this drawing room.

very old is preserved, and the not-so-new is being regenerated. In recent years Lincoln has become less of a backwater, with so much that is altering that even old Lincolnians have trouble finding their way round the ever-changing one-way system, and the recently built bridge and roundabout by the university. Where, by the way, there is a terrific view of the cathedral.

LEFT: The 1810 Judge's Lodgings in Castle Square (left) are used when the Crown Court is in session. In the foreground is a cannon outside the entrance to Lincoln Castle (where the Crown Court and the former County Prison are situated).

RIGHT: Dinner at the Judges' Lodgings is an opportunity to display regimental silver on loan from the Royal Anglian Regiment, 7th Battalion (formerly the Lincolnshire Regiment). The ground floor of the mansion can be hired for private parties, complete with its fine tableware.

BELOW: A medieval week-end in the ruins of the Bishop's Palace recreates the sights, tastes and smells of the Middle Ages. The Bishops of Lincoln had many palaces in different parts of a diocese thought to have been the largest in western Christendom.

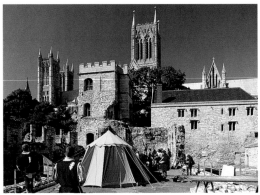

MARKET TOWNS

LUDLOW

Text by Giles Emerson

"It's a bit like France". The flattened central vowel and intonation imme-diately declares: American tourist. You turn to see a pair of chequered trousers topped with a yellow cardigan, accompanying an elegant elderly lady as they disappear down an alley just off Castle Square in the centre of Ludlow. "But isn't this just beautiful," and the voice fades.

It is high summer. Tourist season. The Ludlow Festival of Arts has been over nearly two weeks although the bunting still hangs across Corve Street, one of the main approaches into Ludlow from the north. Castle Square is particularly busy. From it, looking in all directions, you are greeted with

ABOVE: At the bottom of the Broad Street 'promenade' fine Georgian houses surmount a walkway that was once elegantly railed. The 18th century castellated house at the bottom straddles Broad Gate which divides the finer and wealthier residences of Broad Street from Lower Broad Street, former home of cloth industry artisans including dyers, weavers and tenterers.

RIGHT: Ludlow in its hilly landscape, with the castle and church, seen from Whitcliffe Common, which runs to the edge of a gorge above the River Teme. In the background Wenlock Edge runs to the north-east under the bank of cloud.

the prospect of hills and open countryside, views that remain unchanged and that recall A.E. Housman's line about Shropshire's "blue remembered hills". At the western end of Castle Square is Ludlow Castle, a most distinctive ruin, large and imposing, once a Royal residence, now owned by the earls of Powis and meticulously kept – a powerful argument for privatisation.

Taking up most of the square, on an area of functional, unbeautiful tarmac, under an array of green and white striped canopies, is the bustling marketplace. Between April and December, Ludlow market bustles happily on Monday, Wednesday, Friday and Saturday. Usually twice a month, the same stalls are taken up on a Sunday by the antiques and flea market.

ABOVE: This view to the south-west from the tower of St. Laurence's church takes in the centre of the town with Castle Square in the middle and Ludlow Castle against the backdrop of Mortimer Forest, home to about 1,000 deer.

RIGHT: Every year during the two week Ludlow Festival of Arts held at the end of June and beginning of July, an open air Shakespeare play is put on in the centre of Ludlow Castle. Hundreds of people from all over the country come to the performance. Here, professional actors assembled by director, Glen Walford, perform Hamlet.

BELOW: Blacked up for the part, a troupe of Moorish Dancers perform in public in the Castle Square during the Ludlow Festival. Their energetic dance evokes the original Moorish groups who came to dance in Britain and continental Europe about 200 years ago. They dance in front of one of two houses built by George I for courtiers in Ludlow.

Sometimes there are garden fairs here, sometimes book and craft fairs.

Seldom when the sun shines do you see the market empty; even on the non-market days a van selling fish or cheese will usually appear. Ludlow market traders have a businesslike keenness about them. This is mixed with genuine warmth and a slightly bitten look that comes from standing for long periods in the winter cold and damp. The keenest of all traders is Farmers, always occupying the same spot on the north side of the marketplace. This is the most excellent grocer and fruiterer any rural town

could wish for. While you never go short of choice for your traditional fruit and vegetables, Farmers is also adventurous, offering Japanese artichokes, apple bananas from Ecuador, kumquats, generous bunches of fresh coriander, alongside its locally grown tomatoes.

Along with Farmers, Ludlow boasts six good and proud butchers, who vie with each other to win the best sausage competition at the increasingly popular annual Marches Food & Drink Festival. There is also Ludlow Larder, a fine delicatessen, and Broad Bean, a shop selling healthy and organic foodstuffs. Having once been virtually devoid of good things or good

ABOVE: This is typical Ludlow. The timbered facade on the left is Elizabethan, built in 1575 but much of the back part of the house, used appropriately as an antique shop, dates back to the 15th century. Similarly, the Georgian period brick frontage on the right, today the home of the Conservative Association, conceals Elizabethan sections.

LEFT: This flower stall is a regular in Ludlow's open market in Castle Square, and is part of Farmers' popular stall of fruit and vegetables. It appears four times a week in the same place between April and December and three times a week the rest of the year round.

places to eat, Ludlow has become the gastronomic oasis in the Midlands. Top chefs at the Merchant House, The Oaks, Overton Grange, and Underhills are drawing Michelin awards and general acclaim at an equally furious rate.

So there *is* something French about this scene, something to do with food, colours and the movement of people against a backdrop of old buildings in the open air, although the open air cafés are noticeably absent.

Ludlow is one of the most beautiful market towns in England. Most of it is perched on the hill above the River Teme which bubbles with a deal of white water below a gorge to the south-west, bordering Whitcliffe Common and Mortimer Forest. At its centre, looming like a

Left: The Broad Gate, at the junction between Lower Broad Street and Broad Street (partially visible through the arch). A 16th and 17th century house, capped by 18th century 'Gothick' battlements, is built over and round the medieval gatehouse.

Below: Detail of the façade of a three-storey house dating from 1645 at the bottom of Corve Street. Restoration involved removing poorly refurbished panels and replacing these with oak staves and chestnut split lathes to which were added a mixture of clay and sand, with cow dung and horsehair, topped with a thin lime plaster.

Right: Built in 1603 and referred to by Nikolaus Pevsner as "that prodigy of timber-frame houses", the Feathers Hotel on Corve Street is a masterwork of timber motifs, matched on the inside by equally lavish plasterwork adornment. Still a thriving hotel, it is probably the most photographed of all Ludlow's historic buildings.

beacon in every direction, is the large tower of St Laurence's church. The church was started in the 12th century but is mostly 15th century and contains fine effigies of former council grandees in stone, marble and alabaster.

Ludlow is also a place with immense soul.

LEFT: One of a significant number of Grade II listed Georgian houses in Ludlow. Built in 1756, it has recently been restored by the current owners. This view from the rear takes in part of the spacious ⅓ acre garden, framed by old climbing roses.

ABOVE: In the kitchen, the oven is back in the fireplace, now mosaic-tiled but reconverted from a store cupboard by the current owners. The kitchen also has a fine quarry-tiled floor, that had been carefully obscured by several layers of linoleum.

People from the surrounding hills and villages come to shop and do business here; farmers trade their cattle stock at the new market lying just east of the town and only recently moved from a site close to the centre of the town itself. So Ludlow is a metropolis to the locals while it is a haven to visitors from all over the country and abroad, not least to Americans, who only occasionally confuse it with France.

Most of the town is distinctly English, com-

bining Georgian, Caroline, Elizabethan and Jacobean style, sometimes all under the one roof. Broad Street, one of the central streets laid out in a grid pattern in the 12th century, is probably Ludlow's most beautiful street, running from top to bottom with a mixture of Elizabethan wood-timbered houses and shops, and stone or brick houses of the Georgian era. This is reckoned by Nikolaus Pevsner to be "one of the most memorable streets in England". At the bottom

serenity about this performance, with the stage appropriately set against the castle backdrop. When the weather is bad, the same performance is a mass of umbrellas and stoicism. Like a very mini version of Edinburgh festival, Ludlow has its own fringe, best exampled by the Old Dick Theatre Group who perform a bawdy and merciless rendition of the prevailing Shakespeare production in the forecourt of the Bull Hotel.

LEFT, BELOW AND RIGHT: All the rooms in this Georgian house have fine proportions and most have original plaster and woodwork. In this sitting room (right and below) and dining room (left), the owners uncovered and completely renovated the fireplaces and have used bold colour schemes to show up the fine plasterwork on the walls.

is Broad Gate, one of seven original gates in the old town wall that are more or less intact. There are approaching 700 buildings in Ludlow that are listed as of historic or architectural interest; not a bad record given a population of just 8,000.

Many of these buildings are fine, even splendid. They are the legacy of different periods of prosperity in Ludlow, including a highly successful medieval woollen trade and subsequent periods when Ludlow prospered from industries including corn-milling, paper-making and manufacture of woollen cloth and blankets. In the 17th century, the glove-making industry alone in Ludlow employed 1,000 people. When Sir Henry Sydney, one of Elizabeth I's most magnificent ministers, transformed the castle into a palace, Ludlow became almost the literary capital of England. It was already a centre of power with the castle holding the Court of the Marches. Surrounding landowners came to set up house here, forming a wealthy society enjoying balls, masques and entertainments.

For two full weeks in the summer, Ludlow Festival draws crowds from all over the country to enjoy music, literature, opera, ballet, children's events and fireworks at the castle. The main attraction is an annual production of a Shakespeare play, which takes place in the open air, each evening, in the centre of the castle. On a fine, warm summer evening, there is a timeless

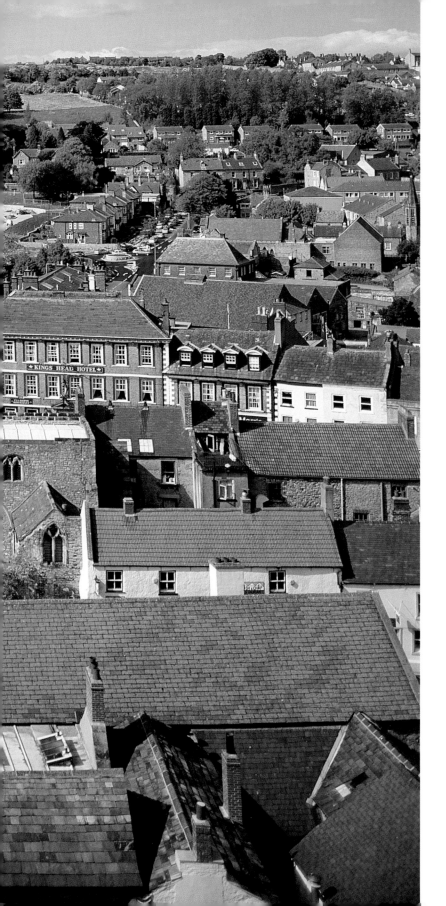

MARKET TOWNS

RICHMOND

NORTH YORKSHIRE

Text by Jane Hatcher

Richmond's splendid Norman castle was one of the first in the country to be built of stone. On a spectacular site high above the waterfall over which the River Swale tumbles, it was built c.1071 by Alan Rufus of Brittany, a kinsman of William the Conqueror. Its magnificent tower-keep, added in the mid-12th century, still dominates the picturesque town which sprang up around the castle. From the keep-top the castle's strategic location, at the junction of upland Swaledale and lowland plain,

ABOVE: A pipe band in the 'Meet' Procession, with the Georgian King's Head Hotel in the background. The Richmond Meet, founded in 1892 as the North Yorkshire and South Durham Cyclists' Meet, is held each Spring Bank Holiday weekend. Its function has broadened to include a carnival procession of floats.

LEFT: Looking North from the top of the Castle keep over the Market Place: the Trinity Chapel is now the Green Howards Regimental Museum; visible above its roof is the King's Head Hotel. The fair visits over the Spring Bank Holiday period. Bolton Crofts, an ancient grazing area still only partly built over, provides a green backdrop.

gives dramatic views of the surrounding countryside. There is also a panorama of Richmond's vast horseshoe-shaped Market Place, originally the castle's outer bailey, and even a distant view of Catterick Garrison, now the largest military base in Europe.

To the south-west the eye scans over the tri-angular Green, medieval Richmond's industrial suburb with riverside corn and fulling mills, tanneries, dyehouse and brewery, and beyond to the eye-catching Gothick folly Culloden Tower, built to commemorate the Duke of Cumberland's victory over the Stuarts in 1746. It is one of few surviving relics of an important

ABOVE: Looking West from the keep-top towards Swaledale. Outside the castle's 11th-century curtain wall, tightly-packed cottages cling precariously to the steep hillside which provided an ideal defensive site. In the left middle distance is the Green, the medieval town's industrial suburb, and beyond that is the V-shaped valley of the River Swale, with Culloden Tower to the right.

RIGHT: The first-floor sitting room in Culloden Tower. Built to commemorate the Hanoverian victory of 1746, this octagonal temple is an eye-catching folly affording spectacular views of the town, as well as featuring in them. Appropriately, it was superbly restored by the Landmark Trust in 1982, as a comfortable and characterful holiday cottage, after a long period of neglect.

BELOW: Overmantel panel in the sitting room of Culloden Tower. This carved wooden panel epitomises Georgian Gothick, a style mixing such classical motifs as egg-and-dart moulding and acanthus leaves with the Gothic ogee arch and satyr's mask. It was repaired in 1982, after vandalism, by renowned York carver Dick Reid.

18th-century landscape garden attached to a since demolished mansion, Yorke House.

Discriminating tourists and lansdcape artists still come to appreciate topography which creates 'picturesque' vistas, and sites of historic interest, including several monastic ruins. Many of today's visitors first experience Richmond from the comfort of the *King's Head Hotel*, behind an impressive list of important eighteenth century guests. The *King's Head* offered well-to-do tourists, in addition to its gracious

LEFT AND ABOVE: The dining room (left) *and drawing room* (above) *of a Georgian house in the town. As well as charming cottages, Richmond has many elegant town houses built by the local gentry, professional men and prosperous merchants.*

RIGHT: Some such houses have attractive period gardens, descending into the well-wooded Swale valley which surrounds the town to the east, south and west.

ABOVE: A flower stall in Richmond Market. It has been the market town of Swaledale for nine hundred years. Each Saturday residents, and others from further afield, buy fish caught on the Yorkshire coast and cheeses such as the famous locally-made Wensleydale, as well as fresh flowers and perhaps some bedding plants.

accommodation, landscaped pleasure gardens known as Plasendale, or Pleasingdale, complete with bowling green and cock-pit. The complex was built c.1720 by Charles Bathurst, whose main seat was at Clints near Marske in Swaledale. Wealthy from mining and smelting lead in nearby Arkengarthdale, he perversely soon afterwards moved to York, and so his newly-built grand Richmond town-house became a hotel.

In addition to the wealth generated by lead-mining, Georgian Richmond prospered from another Swaledale industry, the knitting of the wool from hardy local sheep into hardwearing caps and stockings popular with sailors in the damp Low Countries. Merchants in such commodities, and the local gentry, built their elegant Georgian town houses mainly in Richmond's two most gracious suburbs, Newbiggin and Frenchgate. In the latter is to be found St. Mary's Parish Church, with its monuments and tombstones to erstwhile worshippers, and the medieval choir stalls from nearby Easby Abbey.

Richmond is, however, also a place of charming cottages, which cling precariously to the steep hillside above the river Swale. They housed the burgesses – tradesmen such as carpenters, stonemasons, drapers, taylors, shoemakers, cappers, saddlers, tanners, blacksmiths, maltsters, coopers and butchers. The town's craftsmen banded together into thirteen medieval trade guilds, two of which still exist with the typically quaint names of past trades, the Mercers, Grocers and Haberdashers, and the Fellmongers who were skinners and glovers.

Richmond has many similar anachronistic survivals which continue to enchant visitors, as does its impressive history, charming townscape and spectacular scenery, but Richmond is more

ABOVE: The Market Hall, where an indoor market is held on Tuesdays, Thursdays and Saturdays, with Crafts and Antiques Fairs on summer Sundays. The date of the Market Hall – 1854 – makes it relatively new by the standards of Richmond, where New Road was constructed in the 18th century.

RIGHT: The attractive interior of the Market Hall shows the influence of railway architecture. Richmond had a railway from 1846 until 1969.

than a tourist attraction, it is a place of living and working. The Saturday market is still held, as it has been for many hundreds of years, under the castle's shadow in this small town's vast Market Place, although the three medieval fairs – major trading bonanzas – have long since lapsed. Present-day residents enjoy an immense variety of pastimes and interests, including live theatre at the Georgian Theatre Royal, built by the actor-manager Samuel Butler in 1788 and the country's oldest Georgian theatre still in its original form. Closing in the 19th century as the town's Georgian heyday passed, it endured many ignoble uses, such as a warehouse, but

BELOW: The Georgian courthouse attached to the Town Hall. Above the seat of the Mayor, formerly the chief magistrate, is a royal coat of arms dated 1732 and surrounded by the shields of Richmond's thirteen trade guilds. Other fine early-Georgian fittings include the jury bench and dock. On the far wall are constables' staffs of office.

ABOVE: The interior of the Georgian Theatre Royal. Once seating 400, it now accommodates fewer than half that number in relatively greater comfort, in its original pit, boxes and gallery, all of which are very close to the stage. Providing a diverse programme of drama, music and other entertainment, both professional and amateur, it is an immense asset to this small country town.

RIGHT: Illustrative panel in the Georgian Theatre Museum, representing a typical audience in the 18th century. The well-nourished theatregoers were much more vociferous than today. The Museum also illustrates the working of the Georgian theatre, and contains scenery of 1836, some of the earliest surviving in England.

fortunately relatively little alteration was made, and it was restored and reopened in 1963 to become one of the town's many gems.

In the 18th century itinerant players visited at the time of the annual race meeting, and the former racecourse, now with only the remnants of its handsome Georgian grandstand, is even today used to train racehorses. The Georgian public hall, now known as the Town Hall, and still used for a wide variety of the area's social functions, was then host to assemblies, balls and card parties.

That Richmond is a remarkably well-preserved and charming Georgian town was observed by Sir Roy Strong in "A week in the Country", *Country Life,* 14 July 1994:

Richmond, Yorkshire, has always been one of my favourite towns. There it sits in the middle of the dales looking, at first glance, as though it had been assembled for a child from a cardboard kit. Everything that the ideal Georgian town should have is there, but in miniature: gracious houses, a theatre, assembly rooms, even a winding promenade affording picturesque views... What strikes me most about Richmond is what a monument it is to that 18th-century creed, the pursuit of happiness.

LEFT: Easby Abbey and Church. Many artists have been attracted to these romantic ruins. The Abbey was founded c.1155 for Premonstratensian canons by Roald, Constable of Richmond Castle, from which it can be seen. In Easby church, on the left, are rare early-medieval wallpaintings, and a finely-sculpted cross of c.800.

RIGHT: The Pipe Band Competition, a recent innovation of the Richmond Meet which is held in the Castle grounds.

MARKET TOWNS

SAFFRON WALDEN

Text by Rosanne Kirkpatrick

Saffron Walden in the north west corner of Essex, with its narrow streets and ancient buildings, is one of the unexpected delights of this part of the country. By-passed by the Industrial Revolution, it has retained its medieval centre and original street pattern, and has much to delight the eye in its architecture and gardens.

ABOVE: A view of St. Mary's Church from Gold Street. It dominates the town with its great 19th century spire. This was designed by Thomas Rickman, the architect, who formulated the system we now use in dating and naming the architecture of our churches.

LEFT: Two protagonists from a 1,000-year-old East Anglian legend, on one of the gables of the Sun Inn. Tom Hickathrift, on the left, was a carter of great strength and size (he was six feet tall when only ten years old). The figure on the right is the Giant of Wisbech. He was marauding the Fens and terrifying the inhabitants. Tom was bidden to rid the area of this menace. He made a sword from his axle shaft and a shield from a wheel of his cart and vanquished the Giant.

LEFT: One of the interiors in the eastern part of the Sun Inn, *most of which is now occupied by Lankester Antiques, who also have an extensive stock of second hand books.*

RIGHT: The western part of the Sun Inn. *The date (1676) on one of the gables in the centre is the date of the pargetting (decorative plasterwork), not the structure.*

BELOW: A splendid example of modern pargetting in Castle Street. Some of the designs are created with a block of wood, others are more freehand. It is a craft that is much practised in Saffron Walden and is highly skilled. It is more difficult than in previous times because modern plaster dries so quickly. A plasterer formerly had about 2 or 3 days to complete his work, now it has to be finished within a few hours.

The name derives from the cultivation of *crocus sativus* (an autumn crocus) in great numbers in the Middle Ages, from which the stamens were taken, dried in their thousands and powdered to make saffron. It was used as a dye, medicinally, for culinary purposes and was also supposed to have aphrodisiac properties. The town had been known as Chipping Walden (chipping meaning market), and over the years the name gradually changed, Saffron Walden being written for the first time in Elizabeth I's reign. It is the only town so named in the world.

The most attractive aspect of the town consists of many 500 year old timber-framed houses with decorative plasterwork, known as pargetting, for which Saffron Walden is famous. The plaster in many cases is in pastel colours.

The majority of the other historic buildings of merit were built in the 19th century. This was a time of prosperity in the town for some, because it was by now the centre of the malting industry, using high quality barley grown nearby.

The Gibsons, a family of influential Quaker Bankers, lived in the finest houses in the High Street. They were involved in the installation of many of the facilities in the town. They even contributed to the restoration of the church, for despite the Quakers' cruel persecution some 200 years before, when Wyatt Gibson, then an old man, was approached for a donation toward the rebuilding of the church spire, he replied " Thee ask me for money to rebuild thy steeple? Nay, but I will give thee money to pull the old one down." The graceful spire of the 1830s, which replaced Henry Winstanley's 'lantern', can be seen from all over the town.

The Quaker tradition is still maintained with the Friends' School (which has some 400 pupils,

mostly boarders) and a large Meeting House in the High Street, which has a Quaker burial ground at the rear.

There are many alleyways (known in Saffron Walden as 'twitchells'), leading to small court-yards and gardens. In Bridge End Gardens, a Victorian garden of several acres created by Francis Gibson, there are lawns, a Dutch gar-den, several small buildings, a walled rose gar-den and a hedge maze. The maze was replanted in the 1980s, and runs for about 2,000 feet, a sandy path between high yew hedges.

There is another maze cut in the turf on the Common, not far from the Market Square. This is the largest example of its kind in the world, and one of only eight in Europe. It is in the

ABOVE: A fruit and vegetable stall in the twice weekly market, where local produce has been sold since 1141. During its long history the Market Square has also hosted the burning of a Marian martyr, bull-baiting, a whipping post and stocks.

RIGHT: The 19th century Tudor style frontage of the Town Hall, facing the Market Square, was added to a fine 18th century facade and donated by G.S. Gibson, a wealthy Quaker who was Mayor at the time. The drinking fountain in front has scenes from the Old Testament depicted on its four sides.

BELOW: A detail of the front of the Town Hall: the town crest with supporters of a lion and a dragon. The shield shows 3 crocus plants (the crocus sativus, from which the saffron was obtained and which gave the town its name) within a wall with castellated turrets. It is a pun on the name of Saffron Walden, as it is "saffron walled in".

shape of a four-leafed clover with small mounds in the corners and the centre, and a bank and ditch. If you follow the brick path you will have covered almost a mile.

There is a thriving market in the Market Square on Tuesdays and Saturdays, and it is on these days that buses bring people in from the surrounding villages. The market does not sell livestock any more, but old habits die hard, and there are busy stalls with fruit, vegetables, flowers and plants to be bought, as well as ironware,

LEFT: The former Waggon and Horses *public house in East Street, now a private house. The framed inn sign showing a harvest scene is, unusually, placed actually on the building.*

Mandeville family, and even today there are eight roads radiating from the centre, each named after the first village it reaches, sometimes eight or nine miles distant.

Walden Abbey, also a de Mandeville foundation, was only two miles from the Castle. In 1536 Thomas Lord Audley, the Lord Chancellor, was the lucky recipient of this religious house at the Dissolution of the Monasteries. His grandson, Thomas, 1st Lord Howard de Walden, built Audley End House on the site in the early 1600s.

BELOW: Once the Dolphin *public house, this building in Gold Street still has its sign painted on the exterior. The moulded bressemer beam over the lower window has a dolphin motif along its length. It is now a private house.*

clothes, crafts and books.

It seems a sleepy town but there are many thriving societies, historical and musical in particular, as well as dramatic and women's and men's clubs. There are organisations for all types of sport from indoor bowls to much more strenuous pastimes, and the Lord Butler Leisure Centre (named after the much loved former MP for Saffron Walden, R.A. Butler) is in great demand.

The one comprehensive school with almost 2,000 pupils caters for the children of the town and the surrounding area, with buses to and from the outlying villages. Saffron Walden has always been the focus of the area since the building of the Castle in the early 1100's by the de

Dolphin House

ABOVE: Timber-framed houses in Gold Street, with the beams exposed and coloured plaster between. The overhang of the upper storey is most pronounced and the steps up to the doorways show that the roadway has been lowered.

This great mansion, said James I when he visited, "was possibly all right for a Lord Treasurer, but too big for a king". Later Samuel Pepys was a visitor, and recorded in his Diary that he played his flageolet in the cellars. About half the house was unfortunately demolished in the 18th century. It is now administered by English Heritage.

Saffron Walden is the centre of one of the most attractive and surprising hidden parts of Essex, with many picturesque villages within a few miles, as well as gentle hills which are not often seen in the rest of the county.

ABOVE: A detail of the decorated roof at the east end of the nave in St. Mary's Church. At the top between the angels can be seen a crown, a fleur-de-lys, a tudor rose and a pomegranate. This last was the symbol of Catherine of Aragon.

LEFT: The perpendicular arcade of fine pillars in St. Mary's, showing the pews and clerestory windows.

RIGHT: The South Gate of Audley End, known as the Lion Gate. The gateway was originally Jacobean, and was enhanced in the 18th century with a Coade stone Howard lion on a cap of maintenance, and neo-classical urns on either side.

BELOW: The west (entrance) front of Audley End House, built in the early 17th century when it was a palace in all but name.

CARDIFF

Text by Matthew Williams

Cardiff, the Capital of Wales, is a surprisingly green and pleasant place, full of parks and open spaces but with little left of the industry from which the modern city sprang. During the nineteenth century Cardiff was transformed from a small market town into the greatest coal-exporting port in the world. The coal boom reached its peak just before World War I, but sharply declined thereafter. The city is therefore predominantly Victorian and Edwardian in style, with a wealth of attractive gothic and classical buildings.

ABOVE: The Marquess of Bute was a devout Roman Catholic, having converted at the age of 21. The Castle Chapel commemorates his father, the second Marquess, who created the Docks, and enriched both the town and himself.

LEFT: Dating back to Roman times, the Castle dominates the centre of the city, and is a fascinating mixture of architectural styles. It was the Victorian period that saw the greatest changes, both to the town and the Castle, as they grew rich on "King Coal".

LEFT: A Pompeiian style roof garden is not something one expects to find in South Wales, but Cardiff Castle is full of surprises. One of Burges' happiest creations, the garden was intended as a peaceful retreat for Lord and Lady Bute.

RIGHT: The castle interiors, rich with stained glass, carved stonework and mural decorations, are a wonderful Victorian evocation of the Middle Ages. This is the Winter Smoking Room in the Clock Tower, designed in 1869.

BELOW: The Summer Smoking Room, at the top of the Clock Tower, was the first interior at the Castle to make use of painted tile decoration, as seen here. The paintings, executed in 1874, depict scenes from Greek mythology and the legends of the Zodiac.

Cardiff's origins go back much further. It is nearly two thousand years since the Romans established a fort and trading post near the mouth of the River Taff on the site of the present Castle. Today, the traffic of the modern city

LEFT: The ancient Cathedral at Llandaff was badly bombed in 1941. The extensive post-war restoration included this majestas, sculpted by Sir Jacob Epstein in 1957. Made of aluminium, the magnificent statue completely dominates the nave.

BELOW: The Queen's Arcade is Cardiff's most modern example, but the style clearly echoes its Victorian predecessors. By incorporating different levels this pleasant thoroughfare avoids the claustrophobic feel of many shopping centres.

ABOVE: Today, the bustling Castle Arcade is home to little shops selling the unusual and the fascinating, as well as to cafés and restaurants. Footbridges link the balconies above, where you can find the instrument makers, theatrical costumiers and the like.

rumbles past, oblivious to the original Roman stonework in the walls which once echoed the march of invading Legions. The Norman conquest likewise left its mark on the Castle, which was heavily fortified to repel the indigenous Welsh. Cardiff declined somewhat after the Middle Ages, and became a quiet and insignificant market town, with a small and largely agricultural trade with Bristol, just across the channel.

By the end of the eighteenth century, the industrial revolution had gained momentum in

the mineral-rich valleys of South Wales, and Cardiff began to awake to new possibilities. In 1794, the Glamorganshire canal was opened between Merthyr Tydfil and the sea at Cardiff allowing the effective export of iron and coal.

But it was the local aristocrat, John, second Marquess of Bute, who decided to make Cardiff "the new Liverpool". In 1839, Bute opened the first dock at Cardiff and when the railway was also opened the boom began in earnest. Described as "picturesque but insanitary" in the middle of the nineteenth century, by 1900 Cardiff was a hugely busy port exporting Welsh coal all over the world. The

ABOVE: Cathays Park is home to one of the most impressive civic centres in Britain. The Law Courts, seen here, which date from 1901–5, are a splendid example of Edwardian baroque. Their swaggering style reflected Cardiff's new wealth.

population had rocketed from 3,000 to over 160,000 within the space of the century, whilst in the docks lived a melting pot of people of diverse ethnic origins.

The rising merchant class lived in elegant villas, often in the gothic style made fashionable by the third Marquess of Bute. His architect

RIGHT: The Welsh National War Memorial in Cathays Park is a dignified reminder of the sacrifices made in two World Wars. Designed by Sir Ninian Comper, it was unveiled by Edward, Prince of Wales in 1928.

BELOW: Cardiff became a City in 1905, and this new Coat of Arms celebrated its elevated status. Fifty years later, the City achieved a long- standing ambition and was declared the Capital of Wales.

William Burges had rebuilt Cardiff Castle as a romantic neo-gothic extravaganza, which is today one of the city's foremost attractions. The Bute family, whose name is indelibly stamped upon the city, were fortunately so rich that their urban estate was only partially developed. Vast acres of parkland in the centre of the city, originally part of the castle grounds, gives modern Cardiff a wonderful green lung. Together with the Castle itself, much of this was presented as a gift to the citizens by the Bute family after World War II.

Having grown so rapidly, by the beginning of the twentieth century Cardiff was keen to become the administrative and cultural centre of Wales. In 1898 the corporation purchased Cathays Park near the commercial centre and announced its intention of developing a civic showpiece. It was to have a new Town Hall, the University, a Welsh National Museum, and eventually a Welsh Parliament building. The new and splendid baroque style Law Courts and Town Hall opened in 1905, and the same year King Edward VII granted Cardiff the status of a City.

The first two decades of the twentieth century were years of great prosperity for Cardiff, but a slump began in the early 1920s and trade slid into a slow decline. Fortunately, unlike many British ports, Cardiff escaped the worst of the bombing in World War II. There were some major casualties though, and historic Llandaff

LEFT: In striking contrast to the the exciting modern architecture of Cardiff Bay, the Pierhead Building was built as the Bute Dock Company Offices in 1896. It is now destined to become part of the new Welsh Assembly.

Cathedral was very badly damaged by an enemy land mine in 1941. After the war the city altered comparatively little. There had never been a bad slum problem in Cardiff and, although the usual high-rise buildings appeared in the 1960s, they were few and far between. Much of the old commercial centre remains, with theatres and a major new concert hall, making Cardiff a thriving cultural centre.

The greatest changes have been where the river meets the sea. It was the sea that caused Cardiff to be born, to thrive, and to boom.

BELOW: Exuding Victorian self confidence, The Coal and Shipping Exchange is near the Docks. Built when Cardiff was the greatest coal-exporting port in the world, the exchange still has a commercial use, and makes a splendid venue for functions.

ABOVE: Techniquest is Cardiff Bay's hugely popular science discovery centre. Ideal for children, but just as enjoyable for adults, a range of interactive displays combines learning with fun. There is also a planetarium, and a science theatre for demonstrations.

When the docks lost their importance, the city seemed to turn its back upon them. Much of the old docks area, including once-notorious Tiger Bay, has disappeared.

But in recent years Cardiff Bay has been regenerated and has been described as "the most exciting waterfront in Europe". A barrage has been built across the entrance to the bay, and this will create a marina overlooked by new hotels, shops, apartment blocks, offices and leisure facilities. The proposed Welsh Assembly, envisaged nearly a century before, is also planned for Cardiff Bay. After decades of decay therefore, new life has been pumped into the area. Some of the most innovative architecture of the late twentieth century sits cheek by jowl with the neo-gothic affluence of the late nineteenth. Cardiff Bay is to be linked to the old centre of the city by a new Bute Avenue. This will start from a new public square, and appropriately, at its centre will be a statue of the second Marquess of Bute whose vision founded Cardiff's prosperity. Cardiff is once more reclaiming the sea.

HISTORIC PORTS
CONWY
Text by Margaret Williams

One of Europe's finest examples of a medieval walled town, Conwy has more places of interest packed into a small space than anywhere else in Wales.

Unlike most towns, Conwy was founded on a definite date. Because of his devotion to the Virgin Mary, Edward I chose her birthdate to grant the town its charter. So on September 8, 1284, the borough was created.

Here in this World Heritage site the visitor can walk where kings once trod in the 13th century castle and the even earlier church, experience a shiver or two as he images a shadowy figure slinking by in a stately

Above: Conwy's oldest industry: fishermen Derek Smith (left) and Ken Rimmer Hughes lift mussels off the bed of the estuary against the backdrop of Conwy Mountain.

Left: The castle commands superb vistas of both sea and hinterland. Here one of the turrets overlooks the harbour and the estuary, with the Great Orme in the distance. Edward I always travelled to Conwy by sea for fear of ambush by the Welsh.

LEFT: The kitchen of Plas Mawr, refurnished with a blend of original and replica items, with its massive fireplace where exotic meals were prepared for guests. Fresh milk was provided by Robert Wynne's herd of cows, while spices, sultanas and sugar came from the merchants of Chester and Bangor.

RIGHT: A beautifully carved overmantel, an ornate plasterwork ceiling and heavy oak furniture in the entrance hall of Plas Mawr, the elegant Renaissance town house of the powerful Wynne family, where a bedroom and sitting room were reserved exclusively for Queen Elizabeth I. This room was also used as the servants' dining room and sitting room. The large table and benches are original to the house.

BELOW: The upper courtyard of Plas Mawr showing the stair tower and dignified façades. The house well is in the right foreground.

home, wonder at the minuteness of what is reputed to be the smallest house in Great Britain, and see it all from a river trip where the schoolmaster turned skipper gives an expert commentary and runs wildlife cruises as well.

During the summer festival chapel vestries are given over to art exhibitions, while the

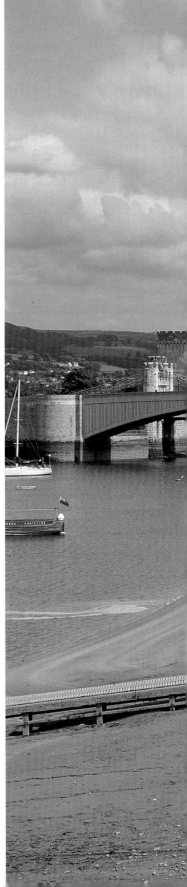

ABOVE: This tiny house on the quayside (left) *is the smallest dwelling in Great Britain. Built in the 16th century it was lived in until 1900, the last tenant being a fisherman who was six feet three inches tall. After being condemned for human habitation it became a showplace and is open to the public today.*

BELOW: The tiny, unaltered upstairs bedroom in the Smallest House.

Civic Hall houses craft fairs and performances by groups and amateur dramatic societies. Youngsters perform their own pageant of Welsh history on the quayside.

Stay for the river festival and explore the quayside where exhibitions of seafaring life are held, or cheer the local fishermen competing at the town regatta.

From the same quay on frosty mornings in winter the mussel-gatherers set out in their small boats for the estuary, their yellow oilskins and multi-hued stocking caps making a colourful splash against the greyness of the turbulent river. Enjoy a dish of mussels in one of the restaurants and you could well find a pearl in a shell – years ago an exceptionally large one was accepted for the Crown Jewels. Alternatively, you can browse in the warmth of the small shops and the comfort of the tea rooms and ancient taverns in the shadow of the 13th century town wall.

All this would have died if Conwy had not met the challenge of the present, combining its traditions and history with a modern outlook and ensuring that visitors come and share in the glorious heritage of the past.

In the Thirties when it was obvious that the age of the motor car would take over, moves were afoot to construct a major trunk road scheme which would have destroyed the harbour. Protestors pointed out that a dual

RIGHT: In the shadow of the castle, King's Quay (right), *built by Edward I, was where trading vessels from European ports used to tie up when Conwy was a thriving port. In its heyday the town had 48 public houses to cater for the large number of foreign seamen and travellers.*

carriageway skirting the town would ruin the unique outlook of the place, and as a result of Wales's largest public inquiry, Britain's first submerged tube tunnel was built under the river, part of a scheme to bypass the town costing nearly £200 million.

Opened by the Queen in 1991, this masterpiece of modern engineering took heavy goods vehicles away from the town and visitors were spared the long wait in queues of traffic.

BELOW: *Veteran musselman Ken Rimmer Hughes who has been working the beds since he was a boy, following a family tradition that goes back hundreds of years.*

ABOVE: *A quick word between mussel-pickers Derek Smith* (left), *Trevor Jones and Francis Smith* (right) *before the laden boats are steered back to the harbour, where the mussels will be cleansed and purified and then sent to the markets in England.*

The tunnel enabled an 80-acre bird sanctuary to be created across the river from the town. The enormous casting basin left after the tunnel had been completed facilitated the building of a multi-million pound marina with berths for 450 boats and a picturesque harbour village near the estuary, bringing fresh life to the town.

It is a far cry from the lonely place it once was, when a group of Cistercian monks decided to build their abbey here. They led their tranquil life in Conwy for nearly 100 years until Edward 1 of England, setting his sights on Wales, wanted their land for his garrison and provided them with an abbey at Maenan, some 12 miles away.

From a remote spot where the chanting of monks and the cries of seabirds were the only sounds that broke the silence, to scene of battle, garrison town and busy port, Conwy has had many roles over the years.

Conwy's importance as a port is indicated by such descriptions as mariner, mate, master or shipwright on tombstones in the churchyard. There were foundries on the river banks, three-masted ships came from over the seas with their cargoes, while men and women continued to

where sloops, schooners and other trading vessels formerly lay at anchor.

Conwy found it had a great deal to offer with its backdrop of mountains sweeping down to the glorious beach, the bustling harbour and the historic houses fronting the narrow streets.

RIGHT: Thomas Telford's graceful suspension bridge. Until this was built travellers had to cross by ferry and endured the furies of the elements. Then a ferryboat tragedy in which ten lives were lost led to the building of the bridge in 1826.

BELOW: The house an Englishman built: Aberconwy House, built in the 13th century and said to be the oldest dwelling in Wales, was the home of an English merchant. The house follows the fashion of the time with the upper storey overlapping the ground floor so as to give extra living space over the storage quarters.

ABOVE: A ruler comes home. From his pinnacle on Lancaster Square, Llywelyn the Great looks out over the town and the church where he was laid to rest, then the Cistercian abbey of Aberconwy. Later his body was removed to Maenan Abbey.

gather the blue-shelled mussels, using the long-handled rakes invented by the Cistercian monks who taught them how to drag the mussels off the sea bed.

Although the mussel industry survived over the years and continues to thrive, the commercial aspect of the port declined with the coming of the railways. But that once despised iron way soon opened the North Wales coast to visitors from England and beyond.

The castle and the other ancient buildings opened their doors to the public, and sailing boats and luxury yachts were now moored

HISTORIC PORTS

DARTMOUTH

Text by Ray Freeman

Dartmouth has been a port for eight hundred years although at the close of the twentieth century its character has changed from earlier days. Whether arriving from the land or by sea visitors are struck by the beauty of the river, sheltered by high wooded hills sloping steeply down on both sides, with the two ancient castles guarding the narrow mouth. The deep water with no sandbar at the entrance remains calm even when gales are blowing out at sea. For sailing ships it has always been the best refuge between Southampton and Plymouth from the prevailing westerly winds along this coast.

ABOVE: Central Dartmouth from the hill above Kingswear, across the river. The blue passenger ferry nears the pontoon where two Red Cruisers are moored. The yellow building on the embankment was once the Station – but it never had trains, which ran only to Kingswear, and is now a restaurant.

LEFT: The boatfloat, seen from the north side, captures the reflections of the dinghies and the buildings behind. On the left is the South Embankment, completed in 1885. Today only small boats which can pass under the bridge can come in here.

After the Normans arrived in 1066 a town was founded, building ships which traded all over western Europe. The seafaring knowledge of a typical "Shipman of Dartmouth" was described in the fourteenth century by Chaucer in *The Canterbury Tales*:

"As for his skill in reckoning the tides,
Currents and many another risk besides
Moons, harbours, pilots, he had such despatch
The none from Hull to Carthage was his match."

The Shipman's modern descendants can be seen in three marinas filled with yachts of all sizes. It was in a Dart-built ship *British Steel* that Chay Blyth set off in 1970 to sail round the world against all the prevailing winds. For those who wish to enjoy the view without effort there are the bright blue or red tripper boats which take visitors out to the Castle or up to Totnes some way inland.

Kingswear, opposite Dartmouth on the east bank of the river, is the premier port for crab and lobster fishing, its catches valued at 25% of the total for the whole of the UK. With 23 vessels registered there, some sail to the Irish and North Seas for fishing, store the crabs alive in "viviers" and sell them abroad or wherever the price is best. The smaller boats work on the nearby coast, unload at Kingswear and sell live to the locals. They are the last commercial

LEFT: *At the Philip Shipyard and Engineering Works at Noss, the last yard to build ships on the Dart, this vintage coal fired icebreaker* Stockvik *is being made seaworthy to return to Sweden. Glimpsed in the river behind is one of the Red Cruisers taking passengers up to Totnes.*

ABOVE: Britannia Royal Naval College looks down majestically over the river. Completed in 1905 to a design by Aston Webb, it replaced the old ships Britannia and Hindustan for training naval officers, who have included several royal princes. In the foreground is a yacht marina, one of three large ones in the port.

RIGHT: At Old Mill Creek, north of the town, a variety of small boats are brought round on the high tide to be stored or repaired. At the end of the creek is the pink coloured old mill house, dating back to the sixteenth century.

vessels based on the Dart.

Dominating the hill to the north of the town stands Britannia Royal Naval College. Naval officers have received their training there for nearly a hundred years. Visiting naval vessels range from submarines to frigates, many from foreign navies. The college is a major boost to the town's economy.

Yet modern Dartmouth is more than a place for sailors. From every century of its long history there are buildings to be found for those who enjoy to walk. Those castles by the mouth of the harbour were not built just to be pic-

Left: Inside the Royal Castle Hotel an internal courtyard was converted in 1840 into an elegant staircase and sitting area, with the old bells still on the wall. At the same time an extra storey was added to this seventeenth century building, which was originally two merchants' houses.

Below: The Butterwalk, once a market, was built in 1635 for a wealthy merchant in the Newfoundland cod fishing trade. The lavish external carvings of mythical beasts and caricatures of faces suggest that the sculptors were used to carving ships' figureheads and had a sense of humour.

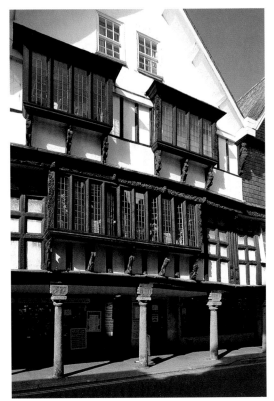

ABOVE: The plaster overmantel inside the Sloping Deck *restaurant in the Butterwalk reflects the strong Puritan element in seventeenth century Dartmouth. It shows the Pentecostal scene, when tongues of flame descended on Christ and the disciples, with Abraham and King David on either side.*

turesque: the first one was designed around 1400 to stop the French, when a chain was stretched across the harbour to halt enemy ships. In the Second World War a boom was stretched across the river, like the old chain, with a steel net to keep out German sub-

marines. In 1944, 495 landing ships and craft left from the Dart to join the invasion of Normandy – it was 1066 in reverse.

In the middle ages the wealth generated from the wine trade helped to build St. Saviour's church. It paid for the gradual recla-

mation of mud from the river into building land on which merchants built fine half-timbered houses decorated with motifs of grapevines and ship's cables. In the 16th century Dartmothians sailed to fish on the Newfoundland codbanks. The next wave of building such as the Butterwalk and Newquay show the profits from dried cod and the

LEFT: The colourful frontage above the China Shop in Fairfax Place, showing the town crest, a medieval cog (cargo ship) carrying the King. The flamboyant carving, reflecting the old Dartmouth style, dates from about 1880.

ABOVE: The Stamp Office originally sold government stamps for legal documents. When built in the seventeenth century it backed onto the river. In the late nineteenth century it was refronted with the bow window and coats of arms of local notables.

RIGHT: This street marks the line of a Foss or dam built across a creek in the thirteenth century to form a tidal mill. Over the years it became a right of way called Foss Street, linking the two parts of the town once divided by water, and is now a popular shopping area.

petition. A Music Festival in May provides something for all tastes. There is a Town Week, a Carnival week and fishing festivals. The Regatta attracts thousands both to watch and take part in the sailing and other waterborne sports. The fireworks and the display by the Red Arrows are the highlights for all. And finally on New Year's Eve there is a fancy dress

BELOW: This "new" Dartmouth Castle was built around 1500, the first in England to be built specially for artillery, to defend the town against the French. In times of danger a chain across the river to a blockhouse in Kingswear kept out enemy ships.

Portuguese wine for which it was exchanged, as do eighteenth century houses on Clarence Hill and in Southtown.

Further silting up of the river enabled the town to build a fine embankment in the late nineteenth century and early twentieth century, as well as to provide a park and gardens filled with flowers in the summer. It is a favourite place for walking and enjoying the river scene.

Some of the old shipyards, cut off from the river, moved to Sandquay up by the Higher Ferry. In 1974 shipbuilding stopped and they were converted into a luxury hotel and yacht marina. The last of the big shipyards at Noss, on the Kingswear side, has done only ship repairs

ABOVE: Looking across to Kingswear from the walls beside Dartmouth Castle. Though it was the first castle built for artillery, the guns soon outgrew its gunports and they had to be placed outside, as seen here.

for the last 24 years but expanded as a marina. However the launching in 1998 of two new trawlers may presage a revival of shipbuilding.

Dartmouth has always had to adapt to changing times. Today its economy is mainly based on tourism. Recently several large cruise liners on tours round Britain have visited the port, where they can put passengers ashore close to the town centre. In the summer months every street is ablaze with flowers as the locals compete in the Britain in Bloom com-

ABOVE: This iron heraldic beast, one of two, ornaments the old door of St. Saviour's church. It looks earlier than the date (1631) below it, which records when the church was enlarged. It may represent a leopard, the emblem of Edward III in whose reign the church was consecrated.

parade round the Royal Castle Hotel and boat-float which brings in coach loads of visitors. Dartmouth has become second only to Trafalgar Square as the "in" place to be.

Yet the river is the centre of all activities now as in the past. One born and bred local says it all: "The river is the mother of Dartmouth. When the river is full, our bellies are full. When the river is empty, our bellies are empty." Happily, the river is still full of pleasure boats of all descriptions, and as a result the people are well fed.

First published in Great Britain in 1999 by

Bouverie House

66 Iffley Road, London W6 0PA

A catalogue record for this book is available from the British Library

ISBN 0 9532771 1 9

Designed by Nigel Partridge

Repro by Dot Gradations

Printed and bound by Arnoldo Mondadori, Italy